SECOND EDITION 6

Student's Book

SUPER MINDS

Herbert Puchta · Peter Lewis-Jones · Günter Gerngross

CAMBRIDGE
UNIVERSITY PRESS

Map of the book

5 In London (pages 58–69) — Why is London famous?

Vocabulary	Language focus	Story	Skills	Think and learn
Shops	Present perfect with *ever / never* Present perfect and past simple	*The Great Fire* **Value** Thinking of others	• Reading • Listening, reading and speaking	Maths: 3D shapes

▶ Song: Have you ...? ▶ Phonics: *s* and *z* sounds ▶ Communication: Get talking ▶ Writing: Think and write

6 Crazy inventions (pages 70–81) — How do inventions help us?

Vocabulary	Language focus	Story	Skills	Think and learn
Tools and machines	*too many / not enough* *Can you tell me what this is / does / is for?*	*Professor Potts* **Value** The benefits of technology	• Reading and speaking • Speaking, listening and writing	Science: Simple machines

▶ Functional language dialogue ▶ Creativity: Get talking ▶ Writing: Think and write

7 This is Houston (pages 82–93) — What do we know about space?

Vocabulary	Language focus	Story	Skills	Think and learn
Moon landing	Gerunds Reported speech	*Alex, the engineer* **Value** Admitting mistakes	• Listening, writing and speaking • Reading	Science: Space

▶ Song: Can you hear us? ▶ Phonics: different spellings of the sound /ʌ/ ▶ Communication: Get talking ▶ Writing: Think and write

8 A cold place (pages 94–105) — What's it like at the Earth's poles?

Vocabulary	Language focus	Story	Skills	Think and learn
In the Arctic	Question tags with *be* *may / might*	*Rescuing the seal pups* **Value** Looking after wildlife	• Speaking and listening • Reading, speaking and writing	Geography: The Arctic

▶ Functional language dialogue ▶ Creativity: Get talking ▶ Writing: Think and write

9 The Jurassic Age (pages 106–117) — What do we know about prehistoric times?

Vocabulary	Language focus	Story	Skills	Think and learn
Natural features	2nd conditional 2nd conditional questions	*The chase* **Value** Taking an interest in nature	• Reading • Listening, reading and writing	History: The Stone Age

▶ Song: I'd like to be ... ▶ Phonics: different spellings of the sound /ɔː/ and question intonation ▶ Communication: Get talking ▶ Writing: Think and write

- **Language focus:** pages 118–127

Back to school

Alex, Phoebe and Patrick are back from their time-travelling adventures. It's lunchtime and they are in the school playground waiting for the bell to ring. They're happy to be back, but they have a strange feeling that something is wrong …

1 001 **Listen and say the words. Check with your partner.**

1 basketball hoop
2 bell
3 net
4 football pitch
5 running track
6 gym
7 litter bin
8 tennis court
9 bike rack
10 railings

2 002 **Read, listen and answer the questions.**

1 What does Alex think is strange?
2 How does Patrick explain their adventures?
3 What day is it?
4 What lesson have they got next?

3 **Choose a word. Draw it for your partner to guess.**

Is that a … ?

1 003 **How much do you remember about the Time Travellers? Do the quiz. Write *t* (true) or *f* (false). Listen and check.**

1 They've already been to Turkey. ☐
2 They've already been to China. ☐
3 They've already had dinner in space. ☐
4 Patrick has already given someone a penknife. ☐
5 They haven't been to Australia yet. ☐
6 They haven't been to the USA yet. ☐
7 They haven't met a famous person yet. ☐
8 Phoebe hasn't bought a city guidebook yet. ☐

2 **Complete the sentences with *yet* or *already*.**

1 He's had breakfast.
2 He hasn't had breakfast.
3 They've seen the film.
4 They haven't seen the film.

3 004 **Watch, listen and say.**

Language focus

Hi there, my name's Leo.
Come in and have some fun.
Have you had some food **yet**?
Are you with someone?

Yes, I know you're Leo.
Because you are my son.
And **we have already met**.
Leo – I'm your mum!

4 **What other things can you remember? Who can make the longest list?**

- What have the Time Travellers already done?
- What haven't the Time Travellers done yet?

They've already travelled on the Turkish underground.
They haven't seen a dinosaur yet.

1 005 **Listen and number the people and the places. Then sing the song.**

a a rainforest ☐

b robbers, cowboys and the sheriff ☐

c a 1950s music star ☐

d a mysterious ship ☐

e a restaurant at the edge of the universe ☐

f a town in Ancient Italy ☐

They've already been to Pompeii
And seen fights in the old Wild West
And they've been lost at sea
On board the *Mary Celeste*.

They've already talked to Elvis
And had some cake in space.
They've walked in the rainforest –
A really amazing place!

Have they been to Africa?
Will they go there? Yes or no?
Come along and let's find out
The places where they'll go.

The Time Travellers –
They're lost in time.
They'll never come back
If they cross that line.

The Time Travellers –
Travelling so fast.
The past is the present
And the future is the past.

Phonics

2 007 **Listen and say the dialogue.**

Patrick It's nice to follow the light through time.

Phoebe Nice? It's exciting!

Patrick And the cake in space was tasty.

Phoebe Tasty? It was amazing!

1 Read the dialogue and answer the questions.

Pepe Did you enjoy the Time Travellers' story in *Super Minds 5*?
Ana Yes, I did. My favourite episode was the one in the rainforest.
Pepe Was that the place where they had to jump off the waterfall?
Ana Yes, that's right. What was your favourite?
Pepe I liked the episode when they met Elvis.

Ana That was good too.
Pepe I also liked the one about the *Mary Celeste*.
Ana The ship which disappeared?
Pepe Well, the ship didn't disappear. The captain and the sailors disappeared.

Ana Ah yes, that's right. Who's your favourite character?
Pepe I like Patrick, the boy who always wants to do brave things.
Ana I like Phoebe because she's the one who always knows where they are.
Pepe Do you think they're going to do more time travel in this book?
Ana I hope they do.

1 What was Ana's favourite episode?
2 What was Pepe's favourite episode?
3 Who was Ana's favourite character?
4 Who was Pepe's favourite character?

2 Complete the sentences with *which*, *who* or *where*.

1 The *Mary Celeste* is the ship ______________ disappeared.
2 Phoebe is the one ______________ always knows where they are.
3 The rainforest is the place ______________ they jumped off the waterfall.

3 008 Watch, listen and say.

Language focus

My name's Leo and I'm a leopard.
I'm the leopard **who** likes to rap.
These are the words **which** I rap.
I'll keep rapping while you clap.

This is the jungle **where** I rule.
This is the jungle **where** I'm king.
King of the jungle, king of cool.
You keep clapping while I sing.

4 Complete the sentences. Compare with your partner.

1 Istanbul is the city where ______________.
2 Alex is the Time Traveller who ______________.
3 The gate is the thing which ______________.
4 Patrick is the one who ______________.
5 Pompeii is the place where ______________.
6 A penknife is the present which ______________.

BACK IN TIME AGAIN

1 **Go through the story quickly and find the answers to the questions.**

1 Why did the experiment go wrong last time?

2 What causes an accident this time?

2 009 **Read and listen to the story to check your answers.**

The children went into the class and they sat down. 'Why did we have to come back in time for a Science lesson?' complained Patrick. 'I don't like Science.' Mr Davis, the Science teacher, walked in and started to explain, 'Today, we're going to do some experiments with liquids and powders and I want you to follow my instructions very carefully.' Alex and Phoebe looked at each other. 'This is strange,' said Alex. 'Yes,' Phoebe agreed, 'and look at the date. It's 1st April. That's the same day that we started our time-travelling!'

Mr Davis told the children to put on their aprons and safety goggles. 'What are we going to do?' said Alex. 'I'm worried that it's all going to happen again. We're going to have an accident and the yellow light is going to appear.' 'Not if we do things differently,' answered Phoebe. 'Last time, Patrick knocked the water over, so we got the experiment all wrong. We can't let that happen again.' 'How are we going to stop it?' asked Patrick. 'Easy! You're not going to do any of the experiments!' answered Phoebe. 'That's not fair!' Patrick protested. 'It's boring doing nothing!'

The children went back to their desks. 'Sit there,' Phoebe said to Patrick, 'and don't touch anything!' Patrick sat down and he took off his goggles. Alex and Phoebe started doing the experiments. They did the experiment which made the brick change colour and then they did the next one, which made the brick get bigger. 'OK. Time for the last experiment,' said Alex. 'Let's read the instructions very carefully.'

They mixed the blue powder, the orange powder and the right amount of green powder. Then they carefully measured the green liquid and they put the mixture down on the desk.

Just then, Mr Davis came up to them. 'Everything OK?' he asked. 'Yes,' said Phoebe, 'we're fine.' 'Excellent,' said Mr Davis and then he looked at Patrick. 'Stop fiddling with your safety goggles and put them on, please.'

Patrick started to put his goggles on, but they went flying up into the air and hit the big jar of blue powder at the front of the shelf above the desk. The jar fell over and all the powder started to fall down into the mixture on the desk below. 'Oh dear … ,' said Patrick.

Suddenly there was a big explosion. 'Oh no! What have you done?' shouted Phoebe. 'I'm sorry,' answered Patrick. 'It was an accident.' At that moment, the yellow light appeared and started to glow. The children looked at each other. 'Shall we … ?' Phoebe started to say. Alex looked into the light and then back at his friends. 'What will happen if … ?' They all knew what they had to do. Together they walked into the light. They were gone in a flash!

3 Answer the questions.

1 Who doesn't like Science?
2 What's the date?
3 What do they put on before they do their experiment?
4 Who doesn't help with the experiments?
5 What did the goggles hit?
6 Where did Alex, Phoebe and Patrick go?

4 Who do you think says these things?

1 'Go and get your aprons.'
2 'You always think it's my fault.'
3 'Please read the instructions very carefully.'
4 'How many spoons of orange powder do we need, Alex?'
5 'Can you pass me the green liquid, Phoebe?'
6 'Science is boring.'

1 The treasure

There were lots of pirates in the Caribbean Sea from around 1500 until the 1700s. The pirates robbed lots of ships, but they didn't always steal gold coins and jewels. Very often they stole food, water, weapons and clothing. They even stole things like soap, ropes and anchors. Sometimes they used to keep the ship which they captured and then sell it. On other occasions, they kept the ship because it was better than theirs.

1 010 **Listen and say the words. Check with your partner.**

1 palm tree
2 hook
3 eye-patch
4 binoculars
5 key
6 hammock
7 coins
8 spade
9 treasure chest
10 hole
11 stone

BIG QUESTION **What kinds of treasure are there?**

2 011 **Read, listen and complete the sentences.**

1 The treasure chest is full of ______________.
2 The pirates are ______________ the treasure.
3 The captain has got a ______________ and a ______________.
4 The children plan to ______________ the treasure.

3 **Choose a word. Mime it for your partner to guess.**

Look! Can you guess the word?

I'm not sure. Is it ... ?

1 Read the magazine article and match the names with the jobs.

Film director Bruce Stevens has been in the Caribbean for more than six months now.

His new project is a film about the famous French pirate Jean Fleury, who robbed a Spanish ship around 1523. 'I've loved pirates since I was ten,' explains Bruce. Jack Collins is playing the part of Jean Fleury. 'I've known Jack for almost ten years,' Bruce tells us. 'He's a great friend and he's perfect for the part.'

1 Bruce Stevens	a a pirate
2 Jack Collins	b a film director
3 Jean Fleury	c an actor

2 Complete the sentences with words from the article.

1 Bruce has ________________ since he was ten.

2 Bruce has ________________ for almost ten years.

3 012 Watch, listen and say.

Language focus

I've had these lovely spots **since** I was a cub.

I've had my big, long tail **for** eleven years.

4 Play the *for* and *since* game.

1 013 **Listen and answer the questions. Then sing the song.**

1 What bird has the pirate got?
2 Has the pirate got an eye-patch, a wooden leg or a hook?
3 What languages does the pirate speak?

I've known my parrot Polly
Since she was an egg.
I've walked around for years and years
On a wooden leg.

Pirates, pirates, pirates,
Get on board the ship!
It's a pirate, pirate, pirate
Caribbean trip.

I've learnt to say 'We're pirates!'
In Spanish, French and Portuguese.
I've robbed lots and lots of ships
On the seven seas.

Pirates, pirates, pirates ...

I've looked for gold and silver
For years and years and years.
I've found a lot of treasure
On islands far and near.

Pirates, pirates, pirates ...

All about music: REGGAE

In the late 1960s, a new sound started coming from the Caribbean island of Jamaica. It was called reggae and had a very different rhythm from other music of the times. Singers such as Bob Marley and Peter Tosh brought the music to an international audience and these days reggae is popular all over the world.

What I think about this song

It's great. It's OK. I don't really like it.

Phonics

2 015 **Listen and say the dialogue.**

Woody We love finding trea**sure** ...
Polly And being in na**ture**!
Woody Gold gives us such plea**sure** ...
Polly And life's an adven**ture**!

1 Read the magazine interview and correct the sentences.

Carlos Santina is well known on the beaches of Cancún. Most days you can find him there with his metal detector. We decided to find out more.

Q How long have you had this hobby?
A For about nine years.
Q Right. And how long have you lived in Cancún?
A Since 1990.
Q How long have you had this metal detector?
A Since my birthday, six months ago. My son and my daughter bought it for me.
Q Do you always go metal-detecting on your own?
A No, I usually go with my friend Pedro. I've known him since I was ten.

1 The machine in the photo is nine years old.
2 Carlos has one child.
3 Pedro bought the metal detector.

2 Put the words in the correct order.

1 Russia? / How / lived / have / long / you / in ____________
2 known / she / long / has / Brian? / How ____________
3 long / have / laptop? / How / had / your / you ____________

3 016 Watch, listen and say.

Language focus

Explorer	Look at my binoculars. They're my favourite thing.
Leo	**How long have you had** them?
Explorer	**Since** I was thirteen.
Leo	**How long have you been** here?
Explorer	**For** eleven weeks.

4 Write a list of four objects which you have. Look at the pictures or use your own ideas. Then show your partner your list. Ask and answer.

How long have you had your rucksack, Eva?

Since my birthday.

1 **Look at the pictures. What do you think the children do with the treasure that they found earlier?**

2 017 **Read and listen to the story to check your answer.**

'Let's climb that hill,' suggested Alex. 'Maybe we can see if the pirates are still here.' Through their binoculars, they could see the pirate ship sailing away to the south. 'What's that other ship with the red sails and the black flag, behind the pirate ship? I wonder who they are,' said Phoebe. 'Well, we'll never know,' answered Patrick, 'but let's check in the other direction. Are there any more pirates coming?'

They looked to the north, but they could only see a bigger island with a town. 'OK, great,' said Alex. 'No pirates around.'

They walked back to the treasure. By now, they were thirsty, so they cracked open some coconuts and drank the milk. After that, they started to dig up the treasure chest. Two hours later, they pulled it out, opened it with the key which was in the lock and found that it was full of gold coins. 'What are we going to do?' asked Phoebe. 'Well, the treasure's ours now!' Patrick said. 'We didn't steal it!' 'No, we didn't,' said Phoebe, 'but those pirates did. It isn't ours.' At that moment, Patrick shouted, 'A boat!' Alex looked through the binoculars. 'They aren't pirates, I can see some children.'

The three friends ran to the beach and saw lots of families arriving on a boat. They were thirsty and tired, so Patrick gave them some coconuts.

'Pirates have stolen our gold coins,' one woman said. 'We wanted to buy farms in America and now we've got nothing.' She started to cry. 'We watched the pirates hide some treasure and we dug it up,' said Patrick. 'Maybe it's yours. You can have it.'

They fetched the treasure chest and the men loaded it onto the boat. 'There's a town on an island to the north. Go there,' Patrick suggested, 'and I'm sure you'll find a bigger ship to take you to America. But be quick – the pirates aren't far away.'

After the boat left, they found some bananas to eat and when it was dark, they lay down on the sand.

At midnight, they heard some people shouting, so they got up and quickly hid in some bushes. There were three men with torches and, with them, they had the pirate captain with the hook as their prisoner. 'Where did you bury it?' one of the men shouted. 'Over there,' the pirate captain answered, 'next to that tree.' The three men walked over to the tree, but they could only see a big hole.

At that moment, Alex sneezed. Waving their swords, the men ran over to where the three friends were hiding. They grabbed the children and took them to the hole. 'If you don't take us to the treasure, we'll throw you in and cover you with sand,' one of the men shouted.

The three friends looked into the hole and saw a yellow glow. They jumped in. They were gone in a flash.

3 Match the sentence halves.

1 The three friends watch as pirates
2 From a hill the friends watch
3 The three friends dig
4 A boat with men, women
5 The three friends give the
6 At midnight, more pirates arrive
7 The pirates grab the three friends and
8 The three friends

a up the treasure chest.
b treasure chest to the people.
c make them stand at the edge of the hole.
d are burying a treasure chest.
e who want the treasure chest.
f jump into the hole.
g and children arrives.
h the pirates sail away.

4 Read the story again. Think of answers to the questions.

1 What was the ship with the red sails?
2 Why is the captain now a prisoner?

1 Read the magazine article. Write *t* (true) or *f* (false).

THE NEW QUEEN OF SWEDEN

8 year-old Saga Vanecek was playing near her holiday home in Tanno, Sweden. She was throwing stones across a lake. She went into the water to get a stone and felt something strange. It was long and thin. When she looked at it she thought it was a stick. But then she saw it had a handle. 'Daddy,' she said. 'I've found a sword.'

Her dad ran to look at it. He knew it was very old and they decided to give it to an archaeologist at a museum. The archaeologist looked at the sword and knew it was very special. She thought it was about 1,000 years old. But experts now believe it could be even older – perhaps from 1,500 years ago.

The sword is 85cm long. It is made of metal but has wood and leather around it. Even though it is very old, the sword is in good condition. It will stay in the museum near the lake where Saga found it for everyone to see.

Saga, who moved to Sweden from America a few years ago, is enjoying the stories she has seen in the newspapers about herself. One of them called her the new 'Queen of Sweden'.

1 Saga was on holiday when she found the sword. ☐
2 At first, Saga didn't know she had a sword. ☐
3 Saga and her dad decided to keep the sword. ☐
4 The sword is a lot more than 1,500 years old. ☐
5 The sword is now on show in a museum. ☐
6 Saga has lived in Sweden all her life. ☐

2 Work in pairs. Ask and answer the questions.

1 What's the most exciting thing you have found?
2 Where did you find it?
3 How did you find it?
4 What did you do with it?

1 018 **Listen to a radio show about people finding valuable objects and choose the correct answers.**

1 Who found a valuable object?
  a Andy Bookers.
  b Mrs Vincent.
  c Mrs Vincent's daughter, Sara.
2 Why didn't Mrs Vincent know what it was?
  a Because it was old.
  b Because it was dirty.
  c Because it was small.
3 Where did she put the bracelet?
  a In the kitchen.
  b On the tractor.
  c In a box.
4 What did Sara want to do with the bracelet?
  a Wear it.
  b Sell it.
  c Give it to a friend.
5 Who borrowed the bracelet from Sara?
  a Her best friend.
  b Her mum.
  c A teacher.
6 Who bought the bracelet?
  a A rich man.
  b A museum.
  c Sara's teacher.

2 Work in pairs. One of you has found a valuable object. Discuss these questions.

- Where were you?
- What were you doing?
- What time of day was it?
- What did you find?
- How did you feel?
- What did you do next?

3 Act out an interview between the person who found the object and a radio presenter. Use your ideas from Activity 2.

4 Write a story about the object you found.

On Saturday afternoon, I was at my grandpa's farm. I was playing with my dog. He ran behind some bushes and started barking. I went to get him and I saw something shiny. I picked it up. It was a gold watch! I was very excited. I ran to the house to show my grandpa.

PRECIOUS METALS

Where can we find precious metals?

Super fact!
Gold is not always yellow. It can be pink or white too.

1 019 Look, listen and number.

2 **Read the sentences about gold and silver. Write *t* (true) or *f* (false).**

1 Gold and silver are very cheap metals. ☐
2 People use gold and silver to make many things. ☐
3 It's easy to get gold from under the oceans. ☐
4 Gold is a light metal. ☐
5 You can find silver jewellery in Mexico. ☐

3 **Work in pairs. Answer the questions.**

1 Which do you like more – gold or silver?
2 Imagine you find a rock with some gold inside. What will you do with it?

I like … more. I will … with my gold.

Why are gold and silver expensive?

It's difficult to find gold and silver, but people want to use them to make lots of different things. So gold and silver are called precious metals. 'Precious' means expensive and important.

Where can we find gold?

Gold is found all over the world. We can find pieces of gold in rocks. Most of the world's gold is in the oceans but it's very difficult to get it from under the sea. Sometimes, people look for gold in rivers. They pick up small rocks in a pan with water in it. They move the pan quickly. Because gold is heavy, it falls to the bottom of the pan and people can collect it easily. Gold can also come from gold mines underground. People use gold to make things like jewellery and parts of computers.

Can we find silver all around the world?

We can find rocks with silver in them in most countries. Artists make silver into jewellery. Mexico makes a lot of silver jewellery. Silver can be used to make other things too, like coins and mirrors.

4 Look at the list of objects in the table and think.
Decide what the things can/cannot be made of and tick ✓.

	gold	silver	gold and silver	not gold or silver
rings				
modern coins used every day				
old coins in museums				
computers and phones				
digital photos				
dentist's equipment				
sports medals				

5 020 Listen and find out about the things made with gold or silver.

6 021 Listen again. What are they? There can be more than one answer.

1 These are made with very small pieces of silver in them.
2 These are made with gold or silver, or gold and silver.
3 These don't have any silver or gold in them now, but they did in the past.
4 These can have very small parts made of gold inside them.

7 Project Make a poster about gold or silver.

- Find or draw pictures of things that are made of the precious metal.
- Label your pictures and add some information about the things in them.
- Write some sentences about the metal. Where is it found? What is it like?
- Make a frame for your poster with gold or silver paper.

The silver jewellery here comes from Mexico.

Get talking

A show-and-tell

1 022 **Treasure is something special to you. It doesn't have to be gold coins. Listen to Daniel talking about the paintings that he and his brother Christopher did on an Art course and answer the questions.**

1 What is Daniel's treasure?
2 What do they show?
3 When did they paint them?
4 Where are the paintings now?

2 **Give a show-and-tell.**

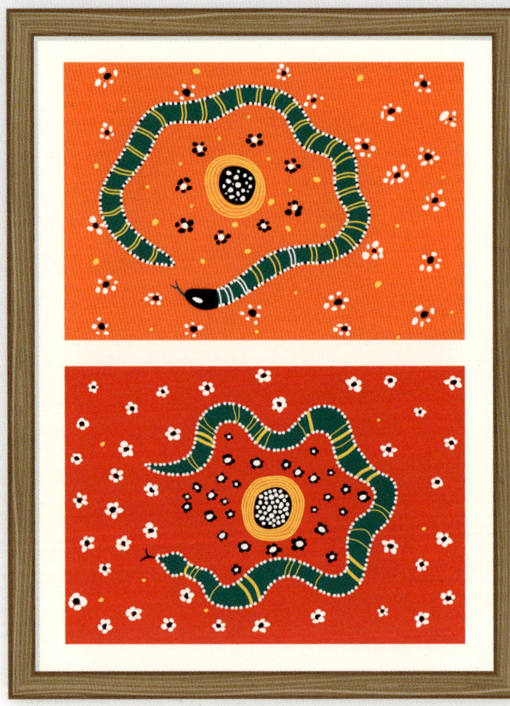

Think about it

- Think about your 'treasure'. It could be an object or a pet.
- Think about why it's valuable to you.
- Think about how to present it. Can you bring it to the presentation or show a photo?

Prepare it

- Think about the questions and make notes.
  - Where did you get your treasure from? Did you get it as a present?
  - Did you create it? Did you buy it?
  - How long have you had it?
  - Why is it important to you?
  - Is it also important to your family?
  - Have any of your friends already seen it? What did they say?
- Decide if you want to show the treasure or a photo of it at the beginning or at the end of your presentation.

Present it

- You should talk for about a minute. Think about questions that you can ask your classmates.
  - What do you think about my treasure?
  - Would you like to see it? (if you have only shown a photo)

Presenting tip

When you finish a talk, say 'Thank you for listening'. Then ask your classmates if they want to ask any questions.

Think and write

A blog entry

1 Start a new portfolio for this year. Write your profile.

2 Look at the photos and read the two blog entries. Who wrote them: Katie or James? How do you know?

Katie

James

MY BLOG

27th March – another great day. I'm so happy. This morning I got a metal detector! It used to be my uncle's, but Mum said he's given it to me! I've already tried it out, but I haven't found any gold yet. Oh, by the way, today I worked with the new boy in our class. His name's James. He's been with us since the beginning of January. I think he's very nice. Tomorrow I'll ask him if he wants to come to my birthday party next week. Do you think he'll say yes?

MY BLOG

Today is 27th March – another boring day for me. I'm writing this in my bedroom. We've lived in this new town for three months now and I haven't made any friends. I've watched twelve films, I've read six books, I've written a lot of emails and I've listened to hundreds of songs, but I haven't made any friends and that's BORING! I've spoken to my dad about it. He says I need to wait. I hope he's right.

3 Read the entries again and answer the questions.

1 What's James' problem?
2 How long has he lived in the new town?
3 What's he done since he came here?
4 How did Katie get her metal detector?
5 Does Katie know James well?
6 What does she think of him?

4 Write a blog entry about today. You can invent the information if you want.

Writing tip

When you write a blog on the Internet, make sure that you don't give your full name, your real address or information about where you live (e.g. opposite Castle Park School).

2 Future transport

1 023 **Listen and say the words. Check with your partner.**

1 hang-glider
2 parachute
3 monorail
4 solar panel
5 microlight
6 wind turbine
7 cable car
8 jet pack
9 surfboard
10 inline skates
11 unicycle
12 floating skateboard

It's the year 2090 and the world's a beautiful place. People have lots of free time and many of them spend it in the big parks which you find in every city. They enjoy doing sports activities. Some of these are very different from the activities that we have today. For example, people don't skateboard any more. Instead they 'floatboard' and it's great fun.

BIG QUESTION **How will people travel in the future?**

2 024 **Read, listen and answer the questions.**

1 Why does Phoebe think that they are in a big city?
2 What does Patrick think about flying a microlight?
3 What do the children decide to do?
4 What does the yellow button on the jet pack do?

3 **Choose a word. Describe it for your partner to guess, but you mustn't use the words *fly* or *transport*.**

It looks like …, but it's got …

1 Read the adverts and complete the sentences.

1. You don't need to know how to fly a plane if you want to use the ______________.
2. You need to have a lot of money to buy a ______________.
3. You need to know how to land when you use a ______________.
4. You don't need to be an acrobat to ride a ______________.

2 Put the words in the correct order.

1. a / to / You / pilot / need / plane / be / a / to / fly / .

   ____

2. drive / don't / car / a / need / to / You / a / helmet /wear / to / .

   ____

3 025 Watch, listen and say.

Language focus

You **don't need** to drive a car to get about round here.
All you **need** to do is climb to get from here to there.
You **don't need** to catch a bus to get about round here.
All you **need** to do is fly to get from here to there.

4 Work in pairs. Make a funny TV advert.

My world: travel

1 **Look at the photos. Answer the questions with a partner.**

1 Which of the types of transport do you use?

2 Which would you like to use more often?

2 026 **Read and listen to the dialogue. Why does Eve like riding a bike?**

Will Wow! That's a nice bike, Eve! Is it new?

Eve Yeah, I got it for my birthday. My old one was too small.

Will Do you use your bike a lot? Mine is somewhere in the garage. I haven't seen it for months.

Eve Yes, I always use it. It's the best way to travel.

Will Really? I don't need a bike. My mum usually just drives me around in the car.

Eve But I can go when I want on my bike.

Will That's interesting! Tell me more.

Eve I don't need to wait for my parents. I can just go.

Will Cool! And they don't mind you doing that?

Eve Well, I tell them where I'm going and when I'll be home. And, of course, I need to wear my helmet. But it's great. And it keeps me fit too.

Will You're right. You know what?

Eve What?

Will I'm going to get my bike out of the garage! I'd like to start riding it more often.

3 **Practise the dialogue in pairs.**

4 **Work in pairs to make your own dialogue.**

1 With a friend, choose one type of transport.

2 Decide why it's good to use this type of transport.

3 Make a short dialogue about the type of transport.

5 **Act out your dialogue to the class.**

What to say

Showing interest

Wow!	Really?
That's interesting!	Cool!

1 Read Jake's post on a forum. Then tick ✓ the true sentences. Correct the others with ideas from his post.

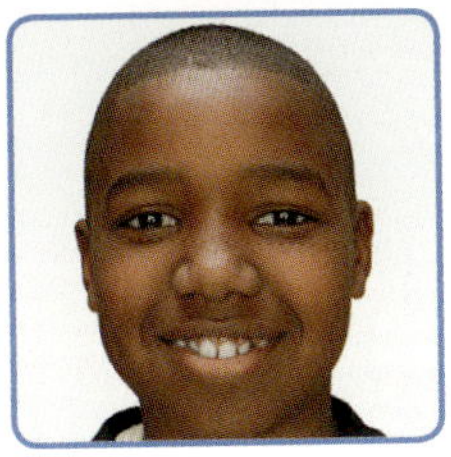

Jake

Thread: How people will get around

Hi, I'm Jake. Of course we don't know how people will get around in the future, but I think there'll be big changes. I think people will move around without polluting the air and transport will be a lot safer than it is today. Cars, for example, will be electric, and they'll be driverless because a computer will drive these cars of the future. There won't be any accidents.

Tell me what you think!

Are these Jake's ideas about the future?

1 There will be big changes in travel. ☐
2 People will pollute the air when they travel. ☐
3 Transport won't be safer. ☐
4 Cars will be electric. ☐
5 People will drive cars in the future. ☐
6 There won't be any accidents. ☐

2 027 Watch, listen and say.

Language focus

There **will** be a lot of noise when the diggers come.
There **won't** be any trees left after the workers go.
I **won't** let that happen. I have got a plan.
They**'ll** have to run away as quickly as they can.

3 Work in pairs. One of you is Jake's friend, who has read the post and calls him to talk about it. The other is Jake. Act out a phone call. Use the ideas to help you.

Friend	Jake
Hi, Jake. I've read your ...	That's great, thanks. What did you think?
I think you're right that ...	Ah, that's interesting.
There'll be ...	Do you really think so?
People will ...	I agree.
I don't think there'll ...	I don't quite agree. I think there'll ...

Do you think there'll be ... ?

Do you think people will ... ?

A PROBLEM FOR PATRICK !

1 **Go through the story quickly and answer the questions.**

1 What happens to Patrick?

2 Who saves him and how do they do it?

2 028 **Read and listen to the story to check your answers.**

Phoebe and Alex read the instructions very carefully. They were both a bit nervous, but they understood how to fly the jet packs now. Phoebe looked up at the sky, but she couldn't see Patrick anywhere. 'OK, this is it,' she said. '1, 2, 3 – go!' Alex and Phoebe pressed the yellow button and up they went. It was an amazing feeling as they went higher and higher.

'Where shall we go?' Alex called out to Phoebe. 'Let's fly to the mountain over there,' Phoebe shouted back. They pressed the orange button to go higher. 'Look at the cable car!' exclaimed Phoebe. They also saw some people climbing, who looked so small below them. 'Isn't this fantastic?' Alex shouted. 'Yes, it's so exciting!' replied Phoebe.

The two children flew twice around the big mountain with their jet packs. Then they pressed the green button because they wanted to fly more quickly. They were heading back towards the park and then past the park towards the sea.

'Hey, Alex!' shouted Phoebe. 'Where's Patrick? I can't see him anywhere!' 'Don't worry,' answered Alex. 'I'm sure he's OK.' Alex and Phoebe flew over the beaches and the sea and then over the fields and the woods. Finally, they followed the river and flew back out over the sea, but there was still no sign of Patrick. Phoebe was getting worried. 'He was too impatient to listen, so he doesn't really know how to fly his jet pack,' she thought.

A second later, Alex saw Patrick. He was high up, but he was falling down through the sky very fast because he had no control over his jet pack. With his arms, he was making movements like a swimmer, but much faster. It looked funny, but Alex and Phoebe didn't laugh. They knew that their friend was in trouble.

'We need to get closer to tell him what to do!' Phoebe shouted. She and Alex stayed side by side. They pressed the orange button and then the green one, to fly up nearer Patrick. Then they pressed the blue button so that they started going down next to him. Patrick looked very scared.

'Quick! Press the yellow AND the blue buttons together!' Alex and Phoebe shouted. They heard a 'whoosh' as Patrick's parachute opened and they knew that their friend was now safe.

As Alex and Phoebe landed safely with their jet packs next to Patrick and his parachute, the man from the jet hire stall was walking over to them. 'Well done, young man,' he said to Patrick. 'I was worried for a few moments, but it's great that you knew about the emergency buttons!'

Alex and Phoebe looked at each other and Patrick was very quiet. He was glad to see a yellow glow nearby. 'Thanks, you two,' he said, as they walked together towards the gate. 'That was close.' Then they were gone in a flash.

3 **Answer the questions.**

1 How did Phoebe and Alex feel about flying the jet packs?
2 Where did they fly first?
3 Why did Alex know that Patrick was in trouble?
4 How many different-coloured buttons did Alex and Phoebe use?
5 How did Alex and Phoebe help Patrick?
6 Did Alex and Phoebe use parachutes?

4 **Work in pairs. What do we learn about the characters?**

1 Why did Patrick not want to get a lesson about the jet pack?
2 How did Alex and Phoebe react when they saw Patrick falling through the sky?
3 Why was Patrick very quiet when he landed?

1 Look at the photos. What do you think is the connection between them?

2 Read the magazine article and check your ideas.

Travelling around Bangkok

Bangkok is one of the busiest cities in the world. More than 2.6 million buses, cars and taxis use the roads of Bangkok every day and it can take hours to travel around in the city. Thai people are always looking for a way to make travelling easier. Here are two great ideas to help with the traffic problem.

One of the quickest and cheapest ways of travelling around the city is to take a Tuk-Tuk. Tuk-Tuks are very easy to recognise because they only have three wheels. The driver sits in a small space at the front and uses a handlebar to steer. The passengers sit in the back behind the driver.

Tuk-Tuks can go quite fast. They will always get you where you want to go quicker than a taxi because the drivers like to drive them in between the traffic on the road. It can be quite scary. If you take a Tuk-Tuk, you should agree the price for your journey before you start – then you won't have to discuss it with the driver at the end.

One of the quickest and cleanest ways of getting about the city is to take the Skytrain. This train looks like something from the future. It runs above the city and the traffic below. The Skytrain won't take you everywhere in Bangkok, but it already has more than 40 stations and carries more than 750,000 people every day. The trains are electric, so they don't cause much pollution. They are also very comfortable and you can usually find a seat.

3 Read the article again and write *T* (Tuk-Tuk) or *S* (Skytrain).

1 You might get frightened on this. ☐
2 It doesn't go all over the city. ☐
3 You and the driver decide how much each journey costs. ☐
4 It's good for the environment. ☐
5 You always sit down to travel. ☐

4 Work in pairs. Discuss the questions.

1 Which of these types of transport would you like to go on most? Why?
2 How do people get about in your town/city?
3 How can people reduce traffic where you live?

1 029 **Listen to the travel stories and write the words under the photos.**

gondola becak pedicab

1 ______________________

2 ______________________

3 ______________________

2 **Work in pairs. Discuss the questions.**

1 How is a gondola different from the others?
2 How is a pedicab different from a becak?

3 030 **Listen again and answer the questions.**

1 What is the problem with gondolas that Anna talks about?
2 Why does Tom prefer a becak to a taxi?
3 What does Emma say about the riders of the pedicabs?

4 **Find out the most popular and least popular types of transport in the class.**

a Work in pairs. Make a list of all the different types of transport that you have been on.
b Think of advantages and disadvantages for each one.
c Put them in order from best to worst.
d Compare your ideas with the rest of the class.

5 **Write a short text about your favourite type of transport. Answer the questions.**

- How often do you use it?
- Why do you like it?
- What problems has it got (if any)?
- How could transport be better in the town/city where you live?

Renewable energy

Super fact!

In Australia, there's a car race for solar-powered cars every year.

What kinds of renewable energy are there?

1 031 **Look, listen and number.**

solar panels

solar-powered plane

wind turbines

battery

biofuel

2 Read about renewable energy. Then answer the questions.

1. Where can renewable energy come from?
2. Why do we use renewable energy?
3. What is *Solar Impulse 2*?
4. Where can you see wind turbines?
5. What is biofuel made of?

3 Read and think. Which kind of renewable energy would be good for where they live? Which wouldn't be good?

1

2

3

WHAT'S renewable energy?

We can get a lot of renewable energy from the sun, the wind and plants. Renewable energy doesn't pollute the environment and we can use it again and again. We can use it to make electricity for homes, schools and other buildings. We can also use renewable energy in batteries. We use batteries in electric cars and other machines.

Sun

The sun makes energy that we can collect using solar panels. In 2016, a solar-powered plane called *Solar Impulse 2* flew around the world in 505 days. This plane had 17,000 small solar panels on its wings. In the future, solar-powered planes will be bigger and faster.

Wind

The wind makes energy too. It can move wind turbines in the sea and on land to make electricity. Wind turbines are very big and one turbine can make electricity for about 500 homes each year.

Plants

We use natural materials from trees and crops to make biofuel. Some lorries, buses and tractors can use this renewable biofuel.

4 Read the two advertisements for transport in the future and match them to the pictures.

Buy a velomobile! It's a car and a bike at the same time. It has solar panels on the roof. When you're tired, you can use the battery. When you want to be healthy, you can ride it like a bicycle. Choose from red, blue or yellow. ☐

Look at these new electric scooters! They're great for everyone and they're very quiet. When you go slowly, you don't use much of the battery. When you go quickly, you use more battery, but don't worry – you can put more electricity in the battery when you need to. Have fun riding about town! ☐

5 Read again. Which type of transport …

1 can be used to keep you healthy?
2 will go further if you don't go too fast?
3 is really two different types of vehicle?
4 doesn't make much noise?
5 can use the sun to make it move?

6 Which would you like to use more: the velomobile or the scooter? Tell your partner.

I'd like to use the velomobile because …

COME AND TRY OUR NEW SCHOOL BUS!

The bus uses energy from the solar panels on the roof. This energy is renewable ☺. Our bus is big and quiet. It can go quickly or slowly. You won't be late to school on this bus!

7 Project Write an advertisement for a new school bus.

- Agree on a type of renewable energy to use for a school bus.
- Make notes. Describe the bus and say what is good about the bus.
- Decide what the bus looks like.
- Write your advertisement and draw it.

Get talking

Hiring a jet pack

1 Work in pairs. Choose a role card.

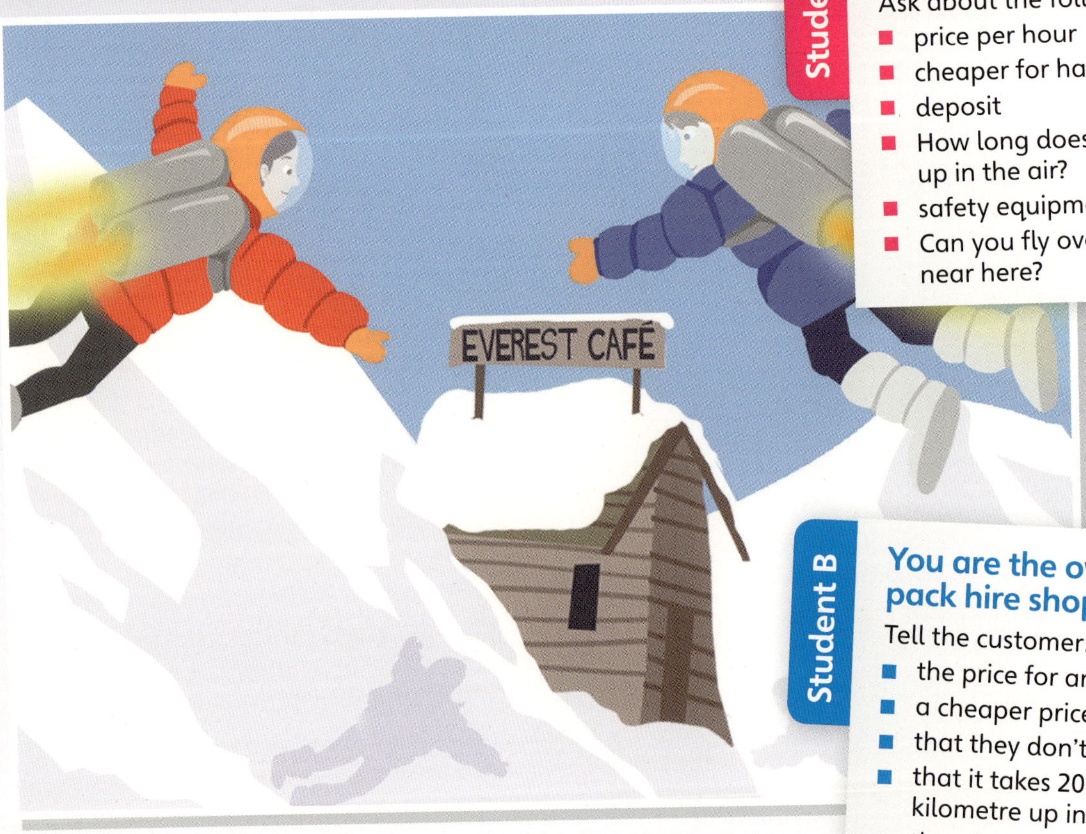

Student A

You are the customer.

You and your friend want to hire a jet pack. Ask about the following:

- price per hour
- cheaper for half a day?
- deposit
- How long does it take to fly a kilometre up in the air?
- safety equipment: parachute and helmet
- Can you fly over any interesting sights near here?

Student B

You are the owner of the jet pack hire shop.

Tell the customer:

- the price for an hour
- a cheaper price for half a day
- that they don't need to pay a deposit
- that it takes 20 minutes to fly a kilometre up in the air
- that they have to put on a parachute and a helmet
- that a very big volcano is about 30 minutes to the south

2 Act out your dialogue.

Student A

How much is it to … ?
What if … ? Is it cheaper?
Do we need to … ?
Do we have to … ?
Are there … ?

Student B

It's … per hour.
If you hire it for …
It will take you …
Yes, you have to …
You'll see …

Think and write

A questionnaire

1 Work in pairs. Ask and answer the questions in the questionnaire. Tick ✓ your partner's answers, not your own.

1 What will a classroom of the future look like?

a There'll be no books, only computers. ☐

b There'll be no classrooms. Students will learn from home. ☐

c Students will learn by downloading from a computer into their brains. At school they'll only play. ☐

2 What will the teachers of the future be like?

a The teachers will be robots, not humans. ☐

b Students will learn at home and parents will be their teachers. ☐

c Children will be the teachers and the students will be adults. ☐

3 How much time will students spend learning every day?

a Students will only do two things in their lives: sleep and learn. ☐

b Only ten minutes every day. The rest of the time they'll have fun. ☐

c They'll spend six hours at school every day, but they'll have lots of homework. ☐

2 Work with a different partner. Tell them what you have found out.

David thinks that in the future there'll be …

He says that the teachers …

He believes that students will …

3 Write a questionnaire about 'Life in the future'.

a Make notes of topics that you could ask about.

food free time
towns buildings

b Write a question for each topic.

What will people eat in the future?

c Write three different possible answers for each question. Try to make some of them funny.

a They'll eat pills and no real food.
b They'll only eat fruit and vegetables and no meat.
c They'll eat the same food all the time: chicken and chips.

Writing tip

When you write a questionnaire, check the word order in your questions.
What will the houses look like?
How much time will people spend at home?
How often will students go to school in a week?

4 Swap questionnaires and answer your partner's.

3 Ancient Egypt

The civilisation which we call Ancient Egypt started in around 3150 BC and lasted for more than 3,000 years. It was very successful and the Egyptians built some amazing buildings, like the pyramids and the Sphinx. The most famous pyramids are the ones in Giza, just outside Cairo. Every year millions of tourists visit them. The rulers of Ancient Egypt were the pharaohs. When they died, people buried them in the pyramids.

1 032 **Listen and say the words. Check with your partner.**

1 Sphinx
2 pharaoh
3 slaves
4 pyramid
5 chariot
6 rock
7 hieroglyphics
8 step
9 mummy
10 tomb

BIG QUESTION What was life like in Ancient Egypt?

2 033 **Read, listen and complete the sentences.**

1 Phoebe has always wanted to see ______________________.
2 Phoebe explains that a pharaoh is ______________________.
3 Phoebe wants to ______________________.
4 Alex thinks that going to the pyramid is a bit ______________________.

3 **Choose a word for your partner to spell.**

1 034 Read the magazine article and complete the sentences with the verb forms from the box. Listen and check.

were taken off | were pulled | were cut | were put

Here is how the pyramids of Giza were built. They were made from big blocks of rock. First, they had to find ways of taking the big blocks to Giza. Here's how they did it:

The blocks **(1)** ________ from the sides of mountains.

Then the blocks **(2)** ________ onto boats and taken to Giza.

The blocks **(3)** ________ the boats and put onto special sledges.

The sledges **(4)** ________ by horses and slaves.

Archaeologists know how the blocks of rock were brought to Giza, but there is still one big mystery. How were they put on top of each other?

2 Complete the sentences with the correct form of *be* and of the verbs in brackets.

1 How ________ the pyramids ________? (make)

2 The pyramids ________ by slaves. (build)

3 The blocks ________ to Giza on boats. (take)

3 035 Watch, listen and say.

Language focus

Who **was** this den **built** by? It isn't very strong.
The walls **weren't built** so well. The windows are all wrong.
The door **was put in** upside down. The roof is not so strong.
This den **was built** by monkeys. It won't be here for long.

4 How did they get the blocks of rock to the top of the pyramids of Giza? Discuss the ideas.

- pull up / with rope
- carry / by slaves
- lift / by UFO

I think that the blocks …

I don't think …

Me too.

I agree. That's a silly idea.

1 036 Listen and tick ✓ the words that you hear. Then sing the song.

pharaoh	☐	tomb	☐	mummy	☐
Sphinx	☐	hieroglyphics	☐	slave	☐

On holiday in old Cairo,
My friend and I went in
A shop where tourists never go,
Which sold a few old things.

We found an ancient mummy there.
I looked into its eyes.
I nearly fell back in a chair.
The mummy was alive!

The mummy didn't want to play.
He was not a happy man.
We left the shop and ran away
And ran and ran and ran.

We stopped and talked to Pharaoh
And asked him what to do.
He smiled and told us where to go.
'Be quick! He's coming after you!'

We ran into a pyramid
With lots and lots of rooms.
We found a dark place where we hid
Behind an ancient tomb.

The mummy came into the room
Inside the pyramid.
He got into his ancient tomb
And we slammed down the lid.

All about music: FOLK

Folk music is used to describe the traditional music of a country, so folk music from England, for example, might sound very different from folk music in your country. Many folk songs are very old and no-one knows who wrote them. They often tell the story of ordinary people who live in the countryside.

What I think about this song

🟢 It's great. 🟡 It's OK. 🔴 I don't really like it.

Phonics

2 038 Listen and say the dialogue.

Enid How was your holiday, Eldrid?

Eldrid Well … everywhere I went, people shout**ed** and scream**ed**. They chas**ed** me all the way home.

Enid Were you frighten**ed**?

Eldrid Frighten**ed**? Enid, I was petrifi**ed**!

1 Read the email. Then tick ☑ the true sentences. Correct the others.

Last week, I went to an Egyptian fancy dress party. A lot of my friends went as pharaohs and a few people went as slaves, but I wanted to go as something different, so I decided to go as a mummy. I spent a little money on some bandages and then I spent a lot of time wrapping them around me. I looked great. There was one problem. While I was walking to the party, it started to rain and I didn't have an umbrella. When I got to the party, I was covered in lots of wet bandages. I didn't look like a mummy. I was a mess!

1 There were more pharaohs at the party than slaves. ☐
2 The bandages were expensive. ☐
3 It didn't take a long time to put on the mummy costume. ☐
4 He was wearing wet bandages when he arrived. ☐

2 039 Watch, listen and say.

Language focus

There were **lots of** trees in this jungle **a few** years ago,
But in **a little** time, **a lot** of them have gone.
We've got to get together to stop this jungle theft
Before it's far too late and there's nothing left.

3 Work in pairs. Take it in turns to close your eyes, point to a picture, open your eyes and describe it.

Number 12 … that's a little money.

THE MUMMY'S TOMB

1 **Look at the pictures and find these things.**

a mummy a scorpion hieroglyphics

2 040 **Read and listen to the story.**

The children walked up to the tomb and looked in through the doorway. 'Let's go in,' said Patrick. 'But what if it's dangerous, or we get lost?' replied Alex. 'Hang on, let's look at these hieroglyphics,' said Phoebe. 'What do you think they say?' 'Welcome?' suggested Patrick. 'It's "Keep out", I think,' answered Alex. 'Well, I'm going in,' said Patrick. 'If I don't come out in a few minutes, come and find me.' 'Don't be silly, we're coming with you,' said Phoebe.

It was dark inside, but they could see a little. They walked for a few minutes when suddenly Phoebe screamed. 'Something fell on my head!' She touched the top of her head and a black creature fell onto the ground and ran away. 'Hey,' said Alex, 'there are more on Patrick's back. And on mine. What are they?' He took one from Patrick's back and looked at it closely. 'Ah. It's a scorpion. There are lots of them. They're everywhere.' 'Scorpions? I hate bugs!' said Phoebe. 'Let's go. Oh, where's that gate?'

The children started running down the dark corridor to escape from the scorpions, but they came to a wall where they couldn't go any further. 'Now what?' asked Phoebe. 'I'm not going back to those scorpions.' Alex was looking at a big button on the wall. 'What do you think this is?' he asked. 'Shall we … ?' But before he could finish his question, Patrick walked up and pushed it. The floor under their feet disappeared and the next thing they knew, they were sliding very fast down a tunnel deep into the pyramid. 'Patrick! Why do you always have to fiddle with things?' exclaimed Phoebe. 'We'll never get out of here!' shouted Alex.

The children landed on a hard stone floor in a dark room. 'OK, Patrick,' said Alex, 'you got us in here. You can get us out.' 'Ssh!' said Phoebe. 'I can hear something coming from over there.' They all looked to where she was pointing. There was something big and white walking towards them. It got closer and closer, holding its two arms out in front of it. 'Run!' screamed Phoebe. 'It's a mummy!' The children ran towards a light which they could see and they found themselves in a small room. 'Quick, Alex,' said Patrick. 'Help me block the door with this rock.'

When the door was blocked, they turned around and looked. They couldn't believe their eyes. All around them, there were gold and silver objects, which were glowing in the sunlight that was mysteriously lighting the room. The children noticed a few hieroglyphics on the walls too. 'Oh, it's beautiful!' gasped Phoebe. 'It's a tomb. I'd like to stay here for hours now.' Just then, another glow appeared. It was the yellow glow of the gate. I don't believe it!' said Phoebe. 'Come on.' The children walked into the light. They were gone in a flash.

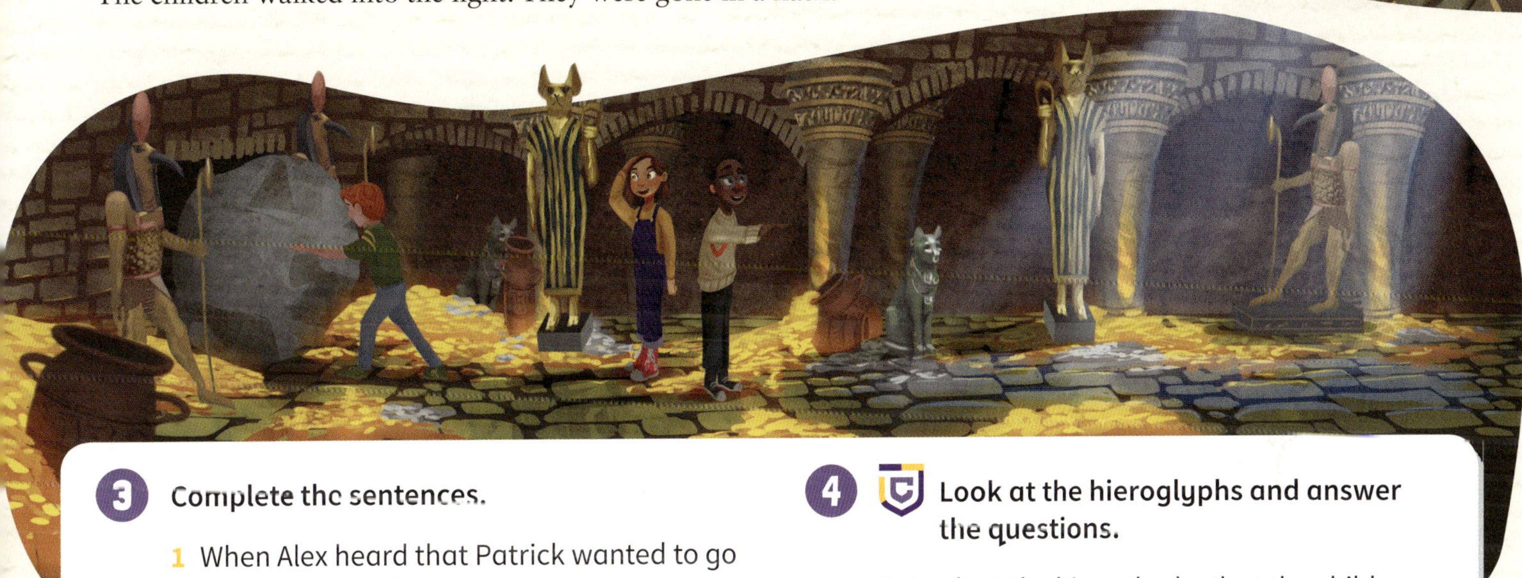

3 Complete the sentences.

1 When Alex heard that Patrick wanted to go into the tomb, he …
2 As soon as they were inside the tomb, they noticed …
3 The children ran down the dark corridor because …
4 Patrick pushed a button on the wall and a moment later …
5 Phoebe got really scared when …
6 Before they saw the gate, the children …

4 Look at the hieroglyphs and answer the questions.

1 Look at the hieroglyphs that the children saw on the doorway. Do they say *Welcome* or *Keep out*? Why?

2 What are these words?

1

2

1 Work in pairs. Describe the hieroglyphs.

It looks like …

It's a kind of …

2 Read the text and draw the missing symbols in the chart.

HIEROGLYPHIC ALPHABET

The Ancient Egyptians had their own alphabet, with symbols which we call hieroglyphs. We can recognise many of them because they are pictures of animals or everyday objects, but some are more difficult to understand.

It is impossible to match the English alphabet with the symbols, but historians have studied for many years to work out the sounds which some of the symbols represent. For example, the hand symbol has a *d* sound and the leg symbol has a *b* sound.

The square symbol is a *p* sound and *r* looks like an open mouth. The top half of a circle represents a *t*, the lion symbol is *l* and *m* looks like an owl.

Some letters have the same symbol, for example, *f* and *v* are both represented by a snake with horns on its head.

3 Look at the pictures. Discuss the questions.

- Who uses this language?
- Have you seen it on television?
- Do you know anyone who uses it?

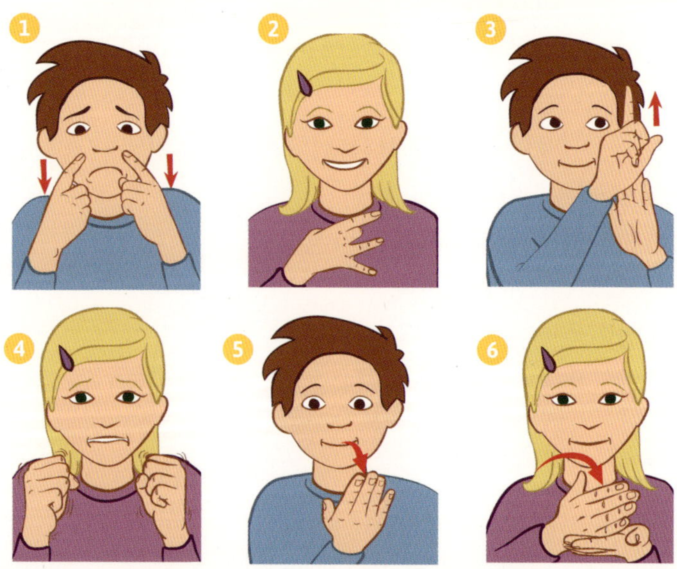

4 041 Match the signs with the words from the box. Listen and check.

tall thank you cry stop like cold

5 Work in pairs. Take it in turns to make the signs and say the words.

1 Look at the pictures. What do you think the story is about?

2 042 Read and listen to the story to check your answers.

The Ancient Egyptians told many stories. Here is one. Do you recognise the story?

1 Rhodopis was a servant in the house of an old man. She was Greek and she looked different from all the other girls in the house, so they laughed at her and called her bad names. However, the old man liked Rhodopis, so the other girls in the house were jealous of Rhodopis and were mean to her. They made her work hard and shouted at her. Rhodopis was very sad about that, but she never said a bad word.

2 The old man didn't know how mean the other girls were to Rhodopis. Her only friends were the birds and an old hippo, and she told them about the other girls when no-one was listening. One day, the old man walked past when Rhodopis was dancing near the river. He thought that such a good dancer should have shoes, so he bought her a beautiful pair of golden shoes. Now the other girls were even more jealous.

3 A few days later, a messenger arrived and told them that the Pharaoh was having a party and that everyone was invited. Rhodopis really wanted to go, but the other girls told her to get on with her work. While she was washing her clothes, the hippo jumped into the river and splashed water over her new shoes. She took them off to dry in the sun, but a large bird flew off with one of them.

4 In Memphis, the Pharaoh was sitting on his throne watching the party. Suddenly a bird flew down and dropped a shoe on him. The Pharaoh knew that the bird was Horus, the God of the Sky, and that the shoe was a sign. He sent for the captain of his royal boat and started searching the country for the owner of the shoe.

5 When the royal boat arrived at the old man's house, the Pharaoh showed everybody the shoe. The girls saw it and knew that it belonged to Rhodopis, but they said nothing. The Pharaoh was leaving the house when suddenly he saw Rhodopis. He invited her to try on the shoe. The shoe fitted and he asked her to be his wife. 'But she's just a servant!' the other girls said. The Pharaoh looked at them 'To me, she is the most beautiful woman in Egypt and she is going to be my queen.'

3 In which part of the story do these things happen? Write the numbers.

a The old man gives Rhodopis a present. ☐
b The other girls were always unkind to Rhodopis. ☐
c The Pharaoh meets Rhodopis for the first time. ☐
d Rhodopis hears about the Pharaoh's party. ☐
e The bird drops the shoe. ☐

4 Work in pairs. Who do you think was invited to the wedding? Why?

1 the old man 2 the other servants 3 the bird 4 the hippo

ANCIENT EGYPTIAN ART

Super fact!

Cats were very important in Ancient Egypt and people think that most families had a pet cat.

What kind of art was there in Ancient Egypt?

1 043 **Look, listen and number.**

sculpture

papyrus

ceramic pot

bright colours

pale colours

2 **Read about Ancient Egyptian art. Then finish the sentences.**

1 Papyrus was made from …
2 Artists used a special liquid to …
3 In drawings, paintings and sculptures, the pharaohs were bigger than …
4 Blue and gold were colours used for …

For thousands of years, Ancient Egyptians did paintings and drawings and made sculptures. Ancient Egyptian art used new colours and had lots of meanings.

What art did Ancient Egyptian artists make?

- Artists did paintings on papyrus. Papyrus was made from the stems of water plants.
- They did paintings on stones. They didn't want the hot sun to make the bright colours pale, so they made a special liquid from trees. They put it on the stones and it helped to keep the colours bright.
- In artists' drawings, paintings and sculptures, the pharaohs were always taller than the other people. This showed how important the pharaohs were.
- Blue and gold paints were expensive, so artists used these colours for paintings of pharaohs but not for other people.
- Artists made sculptures and statues and sometimes painted them in bright colours.
- They also made ceramic pots in lots of different colours.

3 **Imagine you live in Ancient Egypt. Say what art you would like in your house and what material it is made from.**

In my living room, I'd like a … made from …

In my garden, …

In my bedroom, …

4 Look at the pictures and match them with the information.

1  ☐

2  ☐

3  ☐

4  ☐

A There were lots of sculptures of cats. Cats were very important to Ancient Egyptians.

B Egyptian artists used six colours. Each colour often had a meaning: red = being angry; green = being happy; blue = making things; gold = being strong; white = being clean; black = night.

C This important crown was worn by pharaohs. It was called the *Pschent.*

D Sculptures and statues of important people often showed them sitting down with their hands on their knees.

5 Look at the pictures of everyday life in Ancient Egypt and answer the questions.

- What animals can you see?
- What are people doing in the pictures?

In picture one, I can see …

1 

2 

6 Project Design an Ancient Egyptian crown. Describe what it looks like.

- Plan your crown.
- What colours will it be and what do they mean?
- What pictures will be on it and who will wear it?
- Draw your crown and give it a name.
- Write some sentences about it.

This crown is for a pharaoh queen. It's called the Blue Crown of Egypt. It's green and gold because the Pharaoh Queen is strong and happy.

Get talking

A talk about an ancient civilisation

1 044 **Listen to Ellie's presentation about the Vikings and answer the questions.**

1 Why is Ellie interested in the Vikings?
2 In which continent are the countries on the map?
3 What's the special name for a Viking boat?
4 Name three countries the Vikings attacked.
5 Why has Ellie put a question mark under the helmet?

2 **Give a talk about an ancient civilisation.**

Find out about it

- Choose an ancient civilisation and find out more about it. You can use these or your own ideas: the Romans, the Greeks, Native Americans, the Aztecs, the Incas, the Phoenicians, the Aborigines of Australia, the Ming dynasty.
  – Use books and magazines.
  – Go to a library and ask the librarian for information.
  – See what you can find on the Internet.

Prepare it

- Organise the information that you found and make notes.
  – When was the most important time for this civilisation?
  – Where did the people live?
  – What are they famous for? (For example, the Egyptians are famous for the pyramids.)
- Find or draw pictures and maps. Make sure that they are big enough for your classmates to see.
- Use your notes to write your talk. Show it to your teacher to help you.
- Read the corrected text. Then put it away.
- Try to say what you have written without looking back at your notes. Do this until you can talk about your topic easily.

Present it

- You should talk for about a minute, but don't read out your text.
- Use the pictures and maps to make your talk more interesting.

Presenting tip

Don't stand completely still during your talk. When you talk about a picture, point at it. Make sure that all your classmates can see the pictures, so don't stand in front of them.

An invitation

1 **Natalie sent invitations by post, inviting friends to her fancy dress party. Jayden and Emily didn't come. Say why you think they didn't come.**

Maybe they were ill.

Maybe their parents …

Maybe they didn't get the invitation.

2 **Natalie is very creative, so she made all the invitations different. Read the invitations which she sent to Jayden and Emily. Find the problem in each one.**

Hi Jayden,

Please can you come to my fancy dress party? The theme is 'Life in Ancient Egypt'. Please put on an interesting costume. You can come as a pharaoh, a slave or even a mummy!

Time: 6:30 p.m.

See you soon!

Natalie

PS My address:
29 Station Road
(opposite the cinema)

Dear Emily,

Would you like to be someone different for a few hours?
This is your big chance!
I'm going to have a fancy dress party on Saturday 21st April at 6.30 p.m.
I've thought of a great theme, so please wear an amazing costume!
We're going to have hot dogs and fantastic fruit juices.
PS The party is at my place – you know where it is!

3 **Imagine that you are going to have a fancy dress party.**

a Think of a theme (In Ancient Rome, Life in the year 3699, etc.).

b Think what kind of invitations you want to send.

c Decide who you want to send the invitation to.

d Write your invitation. Make it as fun as possible.

Writing tip

When you write an invitation to a party, you need to give the following information very clearly: the date, the time and the place where the party is going to take place. Include a theme if you want people to dress up. Don't forget to sign your message!

4 Olympic sports

1 045 **Listen and say the words. Check with your partner.**

1 long jump
2 hurdles
3 high jump
4 boxing
5 archery
6 wrestling
7 weightlifting
8 rowing
9 gymnastics
10 fencing

The Olympic Games are the world's biggest sporting event and they take place every four years. They are about creating friendship among nations and getting the athletes to compete in a fair way. There are the Summer Games and the Winter Games. Each time the Olympics take place in a different city. Phoebe, Alex and Patrick are in the year 2016 and this time the Olympics are in Rio de Janeiro, Brazil.

BIG QUESTION **What do we know about sports?**

2 046 **Read, listen and answer the questions.**

1 What sports does each person mention?
2 What does Patrick suggest to his friends?
3 Why doesn't Phoebe like his idea?
4 What do they finally agree to do?

3 **Choose a word. Mime it for your partner to guess.**

Look! Can you guess the sport?

Maybe. Is it … ?

1 Jodie and Kyle are at the Olympic Games. They are discussing which events to watch. Complete the programme with the missing times.

Jodie What's the time now?

Kyle 9.50. What shall we go and see?

Jodie Here's the programme. Look, the men's high jump starts in 40 minutes. We could go and see that.

Kyle The high jump? I'm not too keen on that, to be honest.

Jodie OK. We could watch the women's fencing instead.

Kyle Not really, look. It started an hour ago.

Jodie Oh, that's right. Ah, I know. We could go and see the weightlifting. It starts in half an hour.

Kyle Sounds good to me. Let's go!

TODAY'S PROGRAMME

TIME	EVENT	VENUE
(1) ________	Women's fencing	Hall C
(2) ________	Weightlifting	Hall A
(3) ________	Men's high jump	Olympic stadium
11:00	Men's rowing	Lake
11:30	Women's long jump	Olympic stadium
12:00	Wrestling	Hall B

2 Put the words in the correct order.

1 long jump / . / could / and / see / We / go / the

____

2 boxing / . / could / We / the / watch

____

3 047 Watch, listen and say.

Language focus

We **could** play some volleyball, but I don't know how to play.

You **could** try to teach me, but it **could** take all day.

We **could** try some archery, but I'm not so good.

We **could** spend the next few weeks looking in the wood.

4 Write a sports programme for the day. Then swap programmes and decide what to do.

What's the time now?

It's .... What shall we do?

Look. The ... starts in .... We could ...

I'm not keen, to be honest. We could ...

Good idea. / Not really. We could ...

But look. It started ... ago. We could ...

My world: sports to try

1 **Put the sports in the order of how much you'd like to do them. Compare your list in pairs.**

2 048 **Read and listen to the dialogue. Which sports does Miriam talk about?**

Miriam I think we should start doing some more exercise.
Joe Sorry, but I already do enough.
Miriam Really? What exercise do you do?
Joe Well, I walk to school when it's not raining.
Miriam I don't think that's enough. I'm talking about real exercise. We could start rowing.
Joe That's not such a good idea. I'm scared of water.
Miriam Don't be silly. There's a club on Saturday mornings. We could join it.
Joe I don't think so. Saturday mornings is when I do my homework.
Miriam Very funny! You never do your homework before Sunday evening. The club starts at 10 o'clock. I could come round and we could cycle to the river together.
Joe Cycle, then row! Why would I want to do that? That's too much exercise for a Saturday morning.
Miriam Just think how good you'd feel.
Joe Not as good as sleeping in until midday.

3 **Practise the dialogue in pairs.**

4 **Think of a sport you'd like to do. Try and persuade your partner to do it with you.**

1 Choose a new sport that you'd like to try.
2 Write three reasons why it's a good sport to try.
3 Make a short dialogue.
4 Perform your dialogue to the class.

What to say

Turning down suggestions
That's not such a good idea.
Sorry, but …
I don't think so.
Why would I want to do that?

1 Look at the footballer Ricky Oswaldo's organiser. Read the sentences and write *t* (true) or *f* (false).

5G 12:00

DIARY

May

Monday 17th	fly to Rome
Tuesday 18th	train: afternoon
Wednesday 19th	morning: train; interviews 2 p.m. – 5 p.m.
Thursday 20th	morning: train; go to TV studio 4 p.m.
Friday 21st	rest
Saturday 22nd	play: Champions League Final

1 On Monday, he's flying to Rome. ☐
2 On Tuesday morning, he's training. ☐
3 On Wednesday, he isn't training in the morning. ☐
4 On Wednesday, he's giving interviews for 4 hours. ☐
5 On Thursday, he's going to the TV studio in the afternoon. ☐
6 On Friday, he's training all day. ☐
7 On Saturday, he's playing in the Champions League Final. ☐

2 049 **Watch, listen and say.**

Language focus

I'm **running** in the morning
With my best friend Mike.
And on Friday afternoon,
I'm **cycling** on my bike.

Then on Friday evening,
I'm **rowing** here with Ted.
And after that, all tired out,
I'm **going** to go to bed.

3 **Work in pairs. Each of you chooses a famous sportsperson. Write your diary for a week. Then interview each other.**

What are you doing on Monday?

I'm training in the morning and in the afternoon I'm flying to …

What about Tuesday?

I'm … from 10 a.m. to 3 p.m. Then I'm …

And on Wednesday?

NOT THE BEST DAY

1 **Go through the story quickly and find answers to the questions.**

1 Who was hit in the face?
2 Who hurt their foot?
3 Who got wet?

2 **050** **Read and listen to the story to check your answers.**

They took a bus to a sports hall near the Olympic Stadium, where they could already hear the fans cheering loudly and singing. 'Oh, I love sports!' said Patrick. Their seats were in the front row. The atmosphere was already amazing and then when the volleyball match started, what a noise! 'This is great! Much better than watching on TV!' said Alex.

Every time a team scored a point, Phoebe jumped up, clapped and shouted! She was really enjoying it, but two minutes before the end of the game, the ball hit her in the face. 'Ow!' she shouted. 'That hurt!'

When the children left the hall, Phoebe had a black eye. 'You look like a pirate!' said Alex. They all laughed, but Patrick thought, 'I'm glad we're going to the wrestling match now. Surely nothing can happen there!'

At the wrestling, the children's seats were again in the front row. It was a fight between a very tall man and a shorter one. Both wrestlers were good, but the shorter one was fighting very well indeed. After the first period, Patrick turned to the others and said, 'What a great match! But I think the shorter guy will win the fight. He's awesome!'

Just after the start of the second period, the taller wrestler was moving towards the shorter one when the shorter man ran at him very quickly, picked him up and threw him through the air. 'Aagh! Ouch!' shouted Patrick, as the tall man landed on his foot. Patrick held his foot. 'Ow! That's *not* awesome! Come on, let's go,' he said, 'I don't think I'm very interested in wrestling any more!'

The rowing was on a beautiful lake. Phoebe's eye was now more purple and Patrick's foot was hurting a lot, but they didn't complain. 'Are you guys OK?' Alex asked. 'Yeah, don't worry,' Phoebe said. 'I'm fine,' smiled Patrick. 'Well, we're at the rowing now,' thought Alex. 'Surely nothing can happen here.'

Again they had very good seats, near the water. There were eight boats, with four women in each. 'Isn't this great?' Alex asked the others enthusiastically and then the crowd started to cheer. 'One, two, three – go, go, go!' It was great fun, so Patrick, Phoebe and Alex joined in with the crowd. 'One, two, three – go, go, go!'

Alex was so excited that he leaned forward even further. 'One, two, three – go, go, go!' 'Careful!' warned Phoebe. Alex laughed. 'Don't be silly!' he said. Then he started to cheer again. 'One, two, three – go, go', but then with a loud splash, Alex was in the water!

Phoebe and Patrick helped Alex out of the water. Then they saw the gate. As they walked slowly towards it, they looked very funny: one had a black eye, one had a very sore foot and the third one was soaking wet! They walked into the light. They were gone in a flash.

3 **Answer the questions.**

1 How did they get to the volleyball match?
2 What happened to Phoebe at the volleyball match?
3 What happened to Patrick at the wrestling?
4 How many rowers were taking part in the race?
5 How did Alex fall in the water?
6 Why did they look funny walking towards the gate?

4 **Put the sentences in order.**

She only lost one match and that was the Olympic final. ☐
She won the silver medal. ☐
The athlete trained a lot. ☐
Her country sent her to the Olympic Games. ☐
She became better and better. ☐

1 **Look at the photos in the magazine article and find these sports.**

- snowmobiling
- bungee jumping
- BMX biking
- climbing
- snowboarding
- skateboarding

2 **Read the article and match the questions from the box with the paragraphs.**

Why should I go?	How often is it?	What sports do they do?
When did it start?	What are they?	Is it always in the USA?

a

b

ALL YOU NEED TO KNOW: THE X GAMES

c

1 ____________

If you like extreme sports, the X Games are for you. There are two different games: one for summer sports and one for winter sports.

2 ____________

The exciting ones! In the summer games, it's sports like skateboarding, BMX biking and climbing (there has even been bungee jumping) and in the winter games, it's snowboarding, snowmobiling and extreme skiing.

e

d

3 ____________

Every year. The winter games take place in January (or sometimes February) and the summer games usually take place in August.

4 ____________

The first X Games took place in Rhode Island, in the USA, in 1995.

5 ____________

The X Games always take place in the USA. Originally it was in different cities, but since 2003, the summer games have been in Los Angeles and the winter games have been in Aspen. However, there has also been an Asian version of the games since 1998, and in 2010, a European version was started in France.

6 ____________

It's not just a sporting occasion. There's plenty of live music too and lots of fun. It's a great place to meet new people, to talk to the athletes and, of course, to see some great sporting action.

f

3 **Discuss in pairs.**

1. Which of these sports would you like to try? Why?
2. Should all these sports be Olympic sports? Why / Why not?

I'd love to try … because …

I wouldn't like to try … because …

I think … should be an Olympic sport because …

1 Look at the photos. Which human sport is each of these animals good at?

sailfish

kangaroo

elephant

cheetah

puma

2 051 Listen and check which Olympic gold medal each animal wins.

3 052 Listen again and complete the table.

SPORT	BEST HUMAN	BEST ANIMAL
running	(1) ________ km/h	(2) ________ km/h
high jump	(3) ________ m	(4) ________ m
long jump	(5) ________ m	(6) ________ m
weightlifting	(7) ________ kg	(8) ________ kg
swimming	(9) ________ km/h	(10) ________ km/h

4 Work in pairs. Compare your answers.

The fastest humans can run at …

Yes, that's right. And Olympic high jumpers can …

5 Complete the sentences with eight different animals, but don't use the animals on this page.

1 I'm sure I can run faster than a/an ________, but I can't run as fast as a/an ________.
2 I'm sure I can swim faster than a/an ________, but I can't swim as fast as a/an ________.
3 I'm sure I can jump higher than a/an ________, but I can't jump as high as a/an ________.
4 I'm sure I can jump further than a/an ________, but I can't jump as far as a/an ________.

Fitness

How do athletes train?

1 053 Look, listen and number.

weightlifter

boxer

gymnast

rower

fencer

long jumper

2 **Read the fact file about what athletes need to keep fit. Then write the words next to the definitions.**

strength speed stamina balance

____________: someone who has this can do a sport for a long time. They may already be tired, but they don't stop.

____________: someone who has this can, for example, lift up heavy weights or jump very high.

____________: someone who has this can move very fast. This helps them to win.

____________: a person who has this can stand on one leg. You need this to be good at lots of different sports.

FACT FILE

Athletes need to be strong and fast. Weightlifters need **strength** to lift weights and runners need **speed** and strength to win races. Long jumpers need speed and strength so that they can jump a long way. Fencers and boxers need speed to win too. Athletes also need **stamina**. Stamina helps you to do something for a long time. Runners need a lot of stamina to run in a long race, and boxers and rowers need stamina to keep going for a long time. Boxers and gymnasts also need good **balance**. This means that they don't fall over easily.

Super fact!

Running makes your bones stronger when you do it often.

3 **Think of some athletes. Do they need strength, speed, stamina or balance? Tell your partner.**

A footballer needs a lot of …

A hockey player needs …

A … doesn't need a lot of …

4 Which athletes need to be strongest in these parts of their bodies? Put the words from the box in the Venn diagram.

rowers swimmers basketball players long jumpers gymnasts

5 054 Listen to a reporter talking about Valeria Taroni. Fill in the information about her.

Valeria Taroni

1. Sport: ____________________
2. To do her sport, she needs: ____________________
3. When she trains in the morning, she: ____________________
4. She eats: ____________________
5. When she trains in the afternoon, she: ____________________
6. How does she relax? ____________________
7. Why does she love her sport? ____________________

6 Imagine you are an Olympic athlete. Tell your partner what you do and how you train.

I'm a/an … . I train … times a week. In the morning, I …

7 Project Plan and write a leaflet with training ideas for a school sports team. Make headings for the following questions.

- What sports team is the leaflet for?
- How and when do the team train?
- What do they do in the morning?
- What do they do in the afternoon?
- How do they build strength, speed, balance and stamina?
- What do they eat?
- How and when do they relax?

Get talking

Interviewing a famous tennis player

1 Work in pairs. Choose a role card.

Student A

You are a fan of a famous tennis player.

You'd like to ask the following questions:

- When is he/she playing next?
- Where is he/she playing next?
- What was his/her most difficult match?
- Is he/she sometimes nervous before a match?
- Has he/she got a lucky charm?
- How many hours does he/she practise every week?
- When did he/she start playing tennis?

Student B

You are a famous tennis player.

A fan is going to interview you.
Tell your fan:

- when you are playing next
- where the match is going to be
- about your most difficult match
- that you are sometimes nervous before a match
- that your lucky charm is a …
- that you practise … hours every week
- that you started playing when you were …

2 Act out your dialogue.

Student A

Excuse me, may I ask you some questions?
Another question that I wanted to ask you is …
Thank you so much for talking to me.
Oh, just one more thing. Could I have your autograph, please?

Student B

Go right ahead.
No problem. Was there anything else that you wanted to ask?
I'm afraid I've got to go now.
Very nice talking to you.

Think and write

An email to complain

1 Read the email to an online shop and answer the questions.

1 Who is the email from? What do you know about her?

2 Why is she writing?

Dear Toys,

I am writing to you about a game which my dad bought for me from your online shop.

It's the sports game called 'Olympic Dreams'. I wanted it for my birthday, so my dad, Dave Simmons, ordered it five days ago. It arrived on my birthday.

When I opened the box, I found that the 'bronze medals' were missing. Everything else was in the box, but of course we can't play the game without the medals.

Can you send me the missing medals as soon as possible, please?

Many thanks for your help,

Ashley Simmons, 12

Writing tip

When you write an email to a shop to complain about a problem with something, make sure that you get the facts right (for example, the name of the product, the date of the order or when you bought it). Write your email politely and then people will want to help you.

2 An assistant at Toys is reading Ashley's email and making notes on a complaint form. Read the email again and complete the form.

Toys Customer Service

Customer name: (1) ____________________

Order date: (2) ____________________

Problem: (3) ____________________

What we need to do: (4) ____________________

3 How does Ashley connect these pairs of sentences?

a I wanted it for my birthday.
My dad, Dave Simmons, ordered it five days ago.

b Everything else was in the box.
Of course we can't play the game without the medals.

4 What words does Ashley use to make her email polite?

5 Read what has happened and write an email to complain.

You got a tennis racket two weeks ago.
Your grandma bought it in a shop called More Sports and sent it to you in the post.
It broke the first time that you used it.
You don't live anywhere near the shop.
Their email address is mosport@cywi.com.

5 In London

1 055 **Listen and say the words. Check with your partner.**

1 carpenter's
2 jeweller's
3 butcher's
4 grocer's
5 baker's
6 barber's
7 tailor's
8 chemist's

More than 2,000 years ago, the Romans built a city on the River Thames. They called it Londinium. The city slowly grew bigger and richer. In 1600, about 200,000 people lived in the city. It was now called London. In September 1666, a fire started north of the river. The city burned for four days. Almost 80% of the buildings were destroyed. After the Great Fire of London, the city was built again with wider streets and houses built of brick, not wood.

BIG QUESTION **Why is London famous?**

2 056 **Read, listen and complete the sentences.**

1 Patrick is confused because he can't see any ________________.
2 Alex is ________________.
3 Patrick wants to check if the ________________ is open.
4 They find a man and ask him why the shops are all ________________.

3 **Choose a word. Describe it for your partner to guess.**

They cut men's hair there.

Easy! A barber's.

1 Read the magazine interview with a stuntman. Write *t* (true), *f* (false) or *ds* (doesn't say).

INTERVIEWER Derek, I really enjoyed your last film *When London Burned*. Your stunts are amazing.
DEREK Thank you.
INTERVIEWER In the film, you spend a lot of time in burning houses. Have you ever been in a burning house in real life?
DEREK No, I haven't.
INTERVIEWER Have you ever rescued anyone in real life?
DEREK No, I haven't.
INTERVIEWER One last question. Have you ever jumped from the top of your house in real life?
DEREK Again, the answer's no. My real life is very boring compared with my films!

1 Derek's last film was about The Great Fire of London. ☐
2 He has never been in a burning house in real life. ☐
3 In the film, he rescued a lot of people. ☐
4 He has rescued a lot of people in real life. ☐
5 His real life is more exciting than the film. ☐
6 Derek has worked with a lot of famous people. ☐

2 Add *ever* or *never* to each sentence.

1 I have been to India.
2 Have you been to London?
3 Have you met the queen?
4 She has written a poem.

3 057 Watch, listen and say.

Language focus

Have you **ever been** to London Zoo? You've got family there.
Yes, I have. I saw my cousins. They live next to the bear.

Has she **ever been** to London Zoo? Monkeys live there too.
No, she hasn't. She**'s never been**. She doesn't like the zoo!

4 Work in pairs. Have you ever done these things? Ask and answer.

1 go skiing

2 try bird's nest soup

3 cook spaghetti

4 build a treehouse

5 play rugby

6 see a kangaroo

7 visit London

8 do karaoke

Have you ever been skiing?

Have you ever tried bird's nest soup?

Yes, I have.

No, I haven't.

1 058 **Listen and number the countries. Then sing the song.**

France ☐ England ☐ the USA ☐

Have you ever been to London
And walked down Oxford Street?
Don't you think about the people
Who you'll never meet?

Don't you want to travel
And get out of your home?
Don't you know there's more to life
Than being on your own?

Have you ever been to Paris?
Have you seen the famous square?
Have you ever seen the river
Below the bridges there?

Don't you want to travel ...

Have you ever been to New York?
Have you seen the famous zoo?
Have you walked in Central Park?
There's so much there to do.

Don't you want to travel ...

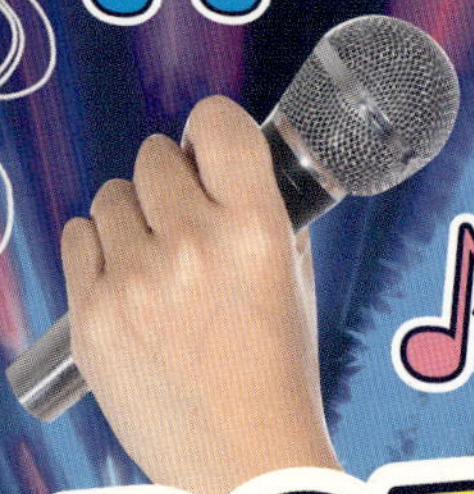

ALL ABOUT MUSIC: POP

There are many different styles of pop music, but the word 'pop' is used to describe any kind of music that is popular with lots of people. TV shows such as *The X Factor* are always trying to find the next big pop star. The words in some pop songs haven't got a lot of meaning, but the songs are popular if the words are 'catchy', or easy to remember, and if it's easy to dance to them.

What I think about this song

It's great. It's OK. I don't really like it.

Phonics

2 060 **Listen and say the dialogue.**

Sam This zoo is amazing. There are so many animals here in the city!

Zara Listen to that hissing. And there's a buzzing noise, too!

Sam Run, Zara! The snakes and bees have escaped from their cages!

1 Chloe is calling her best friend Tara, who is in London with her parents. Read the dialogue and answer the questions.

Chloe Have you been on the London Eye yet?
Tara Yes, I have. I went this morning with Dad, but Mum didn't want to go.
Chloe Why? Has she ever been on a big wheel?
Tara Yes, she has and she didn't like it at all!
Chloe Have you been to London Zoo?
Tara Yes, we have. We were there yesterday. It was great.
Chloe Have you been to Oxford Street?
Tara Yes, I have. I went with Mum. Dad doesn't like shopping.
Chloe Did you buy me anything?
Tara You'll have to wait and see.

1 Where has Tara been in London?
2 Who went on the London Eye with her?
3 Why didn't her dad go to Oxford Street with her?
4 What does Chloe want from Tara's shopping trip?

2 Match the questions and answers.

1 Have you done your homework?
2 Have you ever eaten Chinese food?
3 Have you spoken to Paul?
4 Have you ever been to France?

a Yes, I went last year with my parents.
b Yes, I did it last night.
c Yes, it was delicious.
d Yes, he phoned me this morning.

3 061 Watch, listen and say.

Language focus

Have you ever **seen** the sea?
Yes, I **have**, in May.
I **had** a swim and then
I **went** home straightaway.

4 Work in pairs. A makes a question. B throws the dice and answers it.

visit Mars | make a film | fly a jet pack | eat a lizard | swim with dolphins | ride a giraffe | go to the North Pole | meet a famous film star

- (1) Yes, I have. I did that three weeks ago.
- (2) Yes, I have. I did that two days ago.
- (3) Yes, I have. I did that a year ago.
- (4) Yes, I have. I did that yesterday.
- (5) Yes, I have. I did that five months ago.
- (6) No, I haven't.

Have you ever swum with dolphins?

Just a minute. I'll throw the dice … it's a 3! Er, yes, I have. I did that a year ago.

I can't believe it!

It's true!

THE GREAT FIRE

1 Look at the pictures and talk about what you think happens.

2 062 Read and listen to the story to check your answers.

The children walked along with Mr Fisher. 'The fire started just after midnight in a baker's,' he said. 'The wind was very strong, so the fire got bigger and bigger. The people can't fight it any more and they want to get away. I've just been to look for my brother's family, but they aren't in their house any more.'

At that moment, there was a loud crash as a house near them started to burn and fall down. 'Let's hurry,' said Mr Fisher. 'The fire is getting closer. Come home with me. My wife and our three children are waiting there. We've got two horses and a cart and we want to save our things and then go to my wife's father's house in the countryside. You can come with us. Have you ever been to the countryside?' 'Erm, yes,' replied Patrick, 'I went with my mum to my grandparents' house last summer, but we went by train.' Mr Fisher looked at him. 'By … train? I've never heard of that.' The three friends smiled at each other.

By the River Thames, people were loading their things onto boats. Some people even had their chickens with them. Suddenly Patrick shouted, 'Look at that boat!' Out on the water, a man was getting from a raft onto a boat, where his wife was waiting with their two children and all their furniture. As he stepped onto the boat, it rocked and one child fell into the water.

Patrick dived in and swam. He grabbed the little boy and swam to the boat with him. 'Thank you so much!' said the woman. Then she took off her bracelet and gave it to Patrick saying, 'Please take this!', so he put it in his pocket.

They ran on. After quarter of an hour, they arrived at Mr Fisher's house, where his wife and children were already waiting with some furniture and small chests on the cart. 'Can you help us with this?' asked Mr Fisher, pointing to a very large chest. Together they managed to lift it onto the cart, but it was now very full. 'Everyone get on,' said Mr Fisher. 'We must leave.'

At that moment, a woman arrived with some small children who looked really tired. 'I've found these children. They can't run any more,' the woman said. 'Please take us with you.'

Mr and Mrs Fisher unloaded the furniture and some of the children got onto the cart, but there still wasn't room for everyone. The three friends jumped down and helped the rest of the children onto the cart. 'Go,' shouted Alex and the cart began to move. 'What about you?' asked Mr Fisher. 'Don't worry. We know another way to escape,' Phoebe answered.

There was a yellow glow around the door of Mr Fisher's house. It wasn't from the fire. They walked through the door into the light. They were gone in a flash.

3 **Choose the correct answers.**

1 When did the fire start?
   a Yesterday evening. b At night. c An hour ago.
2 What helped the fire grow?
   a The weather. b Fires in kitchens. c No-one tried to stop it.
3 Where does Mr Fisher want to go with his family?
   a To the river. b To a house in the country. c To the coast.
4 Who did Patrick pull out of the water?
   a Mr Fisher. b Phoebe. c A child.
5 What did the woman give Patrick?
   a Some money. b A piece of jewellery. c Some food.
6 What did the three friends and Mr Fisher put onto the cart?
   a A chest. b A table. c A wardrobe.

4 **Who is thinking these things? When or why?**

1 What does the boy mean?
2 I'm worried. I hope that they're safe.
3 I hope my house hasn't burned down.
4 There are too many things on that boat.
5 This boy is really brave.
6 I hope that there will be room for us on the cart.

1 Read the London information page and match the sentences with the places 1–4.

1 The Tower of London

The Tower of London was built in 1078. First, it was a castle for kings and queens and later it was a prison. The guards of the Tower wear a red and black uniform and are called Beefeaters. Some big black birds called ravens live at the Tower. People say that if the ravens leave the Tower, it will fall down.

2 Tower Bridge

Tower Bridge is one of the oldest bridges in London. Every day, a lot of traffic crosses the bridge. The traffic has to stop when a big ship arrives and then the two parts of the bridge are raised so that the ship can pass. The two parts are raised about 800 times every year. Between the towers of the bridge there is a walkway. You have to pay if you want to go on the walkway.

3 The London Eye

The London Eye is about twice as high as Tower Bridge. From its 32 glass observation pods, you can see the whole of London. The ride lasts about 25 minutes. The London Eye is very popular so there are often lots of people waiting to get on. You have to pay if you want to ride it.

4 Madame Tussauds

Madame Tussauds is the perfect place to take photos next to famous people. Of course, the famous people aren't real. They're all made of wax, but when your friends back home see the pictures, they don't need to know that! It's open every day of the year except December 25th.

a It's only closed one day every year. ☐

b Ships go under it. ☐

c You often have to wait a long time before you can get on. ☐

d Birds live here. ☐

e Cars go across it. ☐

f You can see models of celebrities here. ☐

g Kings and queens lived here. ☐

h It's higher than Tower Bridge. ☐

1 063 **Listen to the recorded message and complete the advert.**

LondonTours'R'us

Are you brave enough for the Dungeon?

- **Come and experience 1,000 years of London's bloodiest history.**
- **Actors and scary rides bring alive many of the capital's most terrible secrets.**

Adults (1) £ ______

Children (2) £ ______

Tours run: (3) ______ days

a week with (4) ______ bus pick-up points in the city.

Phone: (5) ______

2 **Lily meets James when she's on holiday in London. Read the dialogue and complete Lily's postcard.**

James Have you been to Sea Life, the London Aquarium?

Lily Yes, we went there yesterday.

James Did you like it?

Lily Yes, it was fantastic. They have lots of sharks there. We were really lucky. When we got there, they started feeding the sharks. It was really cool.

James Did you also see the green sea turtles?

Lily Of course we did. We even learned why they are green.

James Why is that then?

Lily It's because they eat the green stuff that grows in the sea.

James Really? And did you see the penguins?

Lily Yes, they were my favourites. We went to the ice cave and watched them diving. I love that aquarium. I want to go again.

James Maybe we can go together?

Lily That would be nice, but I'm going home in two days.

Dear Grandma,
I'm having a great time in London.
Yesterday I went to the London Aquarium.
We arrived when they were
(1) ______. That was really cool.
I also saw some (2) ______. Did you
know they get their (3) ______ from
the food they eat?
My (4) ______ were the penguins.
I spent a long time watching them diving in
(5) ______.
Love Lily
PS I've made a new friend. His name's
(6) ______ and he's really nice.

3 **Work in groups. Discuss the questions.**

1 Which attractions in London would you most like to visit? Why?

> I'd like to visit the … because …

> I'm not sure. I'd like to …, but I'd also like to …

> I don't think the … sounds very interesting.

2 Agree on a list of the top five attractions where you live.

3D SHAPES

What 3D shapes are buildings?

1 064 Look, listen and number.

Super fact! There's a lift in the Shard that travels at six metres per second.

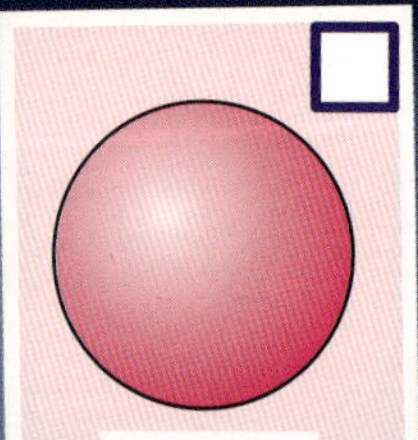
sphere

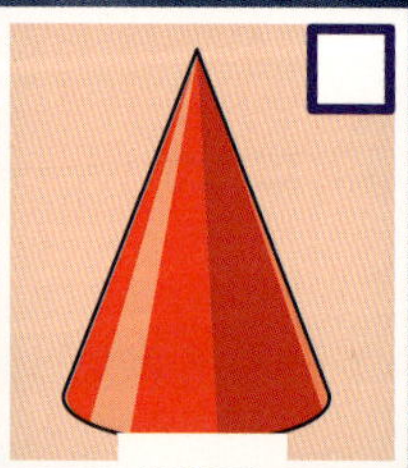
cone

cylinder

cube

cuboid

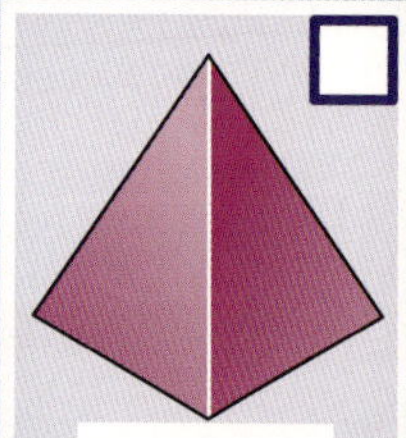
pyramid

2 Read about some London buildings with 3D shapes. Write the buildings' names under the photos.

London is famous for its interesting buildings. Some of the buildings in London are made of 3D shapes. A good example is **The Globe Theatre**. It is actually a cylinder with no roof.

The BT Tower is a very tall cylinder with smaller cylinders at the top. One of the cylinders is a restaurant that moves round and round in circles.

Other buildings are made of than one 3D shape. **Big Ben** is a long cuboid and it's got a cube at the top with a clock on it. There's also a small pyramid-shaped roof above the cube. **Canary Wharf** is also a tall cuboid with a pyramid roof on top. It's got 50 floors.

The American Embassy is a glass cube. **The Shard** is also made of glass. It looks like a very tall, thin pyramid but its sides don't touch at the top. It's got 11,000 windows and 95 floors.

1

______

2

______

3

______

4

______

5

______

6

______

3 Look at the shapes and decide. Which of the buildings are they? Tell your friend.

I think picture a is the …

a

b
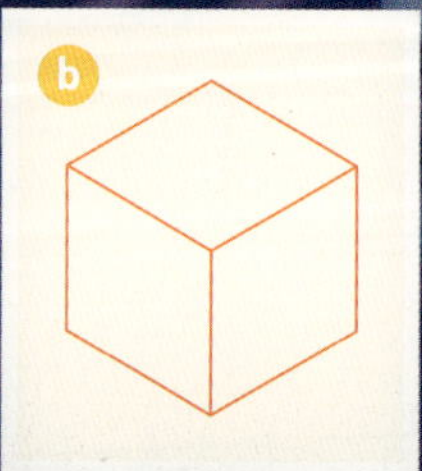

c
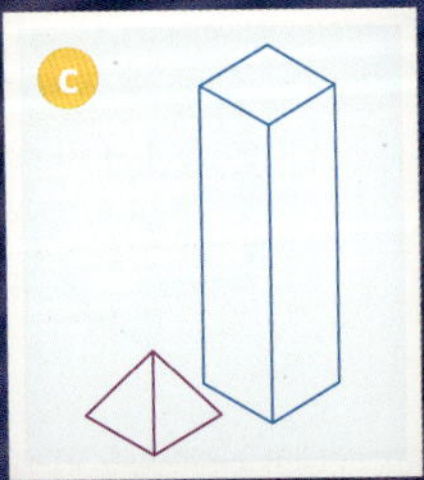

4 Look, read and tick ✓ the shapes in the table.

The Gherkin

The Walkie Talkie

The Cheesegrater

1 This building is tall with a pointed top. It's made of glass and metal. It looks like a cone shape, but it isn't.

2 This building is tall and it has an unusual shape. It looks like a cuboid, but it's got curved sides. The top part is bigger than the part below. It's made of glass and metal.

3 This building is very tall and thin. Its sides are triangles and it looks like a pyramid. It's pointed at the top and it's made of glass and metal.

Building name	3D shape it looks like:		
	cuboid	cone	pyramid
1 The Gherkin			
2 The Walkie Talkie			
3 The Cheesegrater			

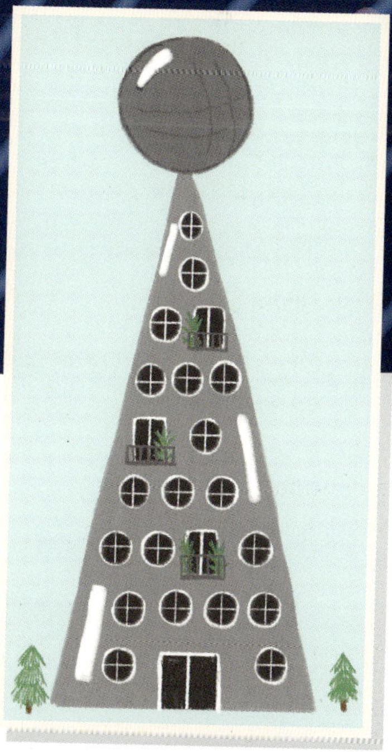

5 Project Design a new building for your school.

- What kind of building is it?
- Which 3D shapes will it have?
- Will it be tall or short?
- What will it be made of?
- Draw the building.
- What is it called?
- Tell your friends about it.

This is the .... It's a ....

Get talking

A group presentation

1 065 **Listen to Alice, Thomas and Emily talking about Sydney in Australia. What do they each talk about?**

Alice talks about … Thomas talks about … Emily talks about …

2 **Give a group presentation about an interesting city.**

Find out about it

- Work in a group of three. Choose an interesting city and find out more about it.
  - Use books and magazines.
  - Ask travel agencies for travel brochures and other materials.
  - Find photos, information, town guides and holiday reviews on the Internet.

Prepare it

- Decide which information each person should look for:
  - what part of the country the city is in (north, south, etc.)
  - famous sights
  - the weather and when it is best to visit
  - languages
  - what people do at special times such as festivals
- Organise the information that you found and make notes.
- Find or draw pictures and maps. Make sure that they are big enough for your classmates to see.
- Use your notes to write your talk. Show it to your teacher to help you.
- Decide what each of you is going to say.
- Try to say what you have written without looking at your talk. Do this until you can talk about your topic easily.
- Practise it as a group. Each of you must know when the other one stops, so that you can continue without a long pause. Decide when to show the photos.

Present it

- Point to your city on the map.
- Tell your classmates about your city and present the photos.
- You should talk for about a minute, but you should try not to read your text.

Presenting tip

Before you start your research, ask other students in the class what they would like to know before they visit a city and take notes. As you plan your talk, check the notes that you took and make sure that you have included all the information.

A postcard

1 **Read the postcards and answer the questions.**

Hi Mum,
Greetings from Brighton.
We're having a great time with Grandma. The weather's fantastic – we haven't had any rain! Brighton's a brilliant town. It's got a very nice beach and the people are very friendly. We've been to lots of shops and we've found some nice souvenirs. We've also bought a little present for you, but sorry … we can't tell you what it is. Just wait and see. It's a secret!
Love,
Freya and Max

Hello Rose,
Greetings from our holiday in Paris. What a great place! I've seen the Eiffel Tower and I've been to lots of museums. (I liked the Louvre best!) I've taken lots of photos too. Guess what? Yesterday I bought a really cool hat. I've made lots of friends here too, but there's just one problem – the weather's rubbish! There's been a lot of rain and it's quite cold.
See you soon,
Amy

1 Who's on holiday in France?
2 Who's had better weather?
3 Who's bought something for someone at home?
4 Who'll bring back photos of their holiday?
5 Who needs warm clothes?
6 Who's made new friends?

2 **Imagine that you're on holiday in London. Think about the questions and make notes.**

- How long have you been here?
- What famous places have you visited?
- What did you like best?
- How has the weather been so far?
- Have you been to any shops? Why (not)? What have you bought?
- What do you think of London?

3 **Write a postcard to an English-speaking friend. Think of a name and use your notes to write to him/her about your holiday.**

Writing tip

We write postcards to friends and family members, so that's why we use very informal language: *Hi! really cool What a great place! rubbish Guess what? Love,*

6 Crazy inventions

History is full of great inventors. Leonardo da Vinci, for example, drew the first plans for the helicopter. Then there was Alexander Graham Bell, who invented the telephone, and Alberto Santos-Dumont, who invented the plane (although some people say that this was the Wright brothers). However, have you ever heard about Professor Potts? He's an inventor from the future …

1 066 **Listen and say the words. Check with your partner.**

1 screwdriver
2 hammer
3 drill
4 saw
5 lever
6 spanner
7 paintbrush
8 paint pot
9 button
10 switch
11 nails
12 workbench

BIG QUESTION How do inventions help us?

2 067 **Read, listen and answer the questions.**

1 What does Patrick think the man at the workbench looks like?
2 What tools does the man ask for?
3 What is the date today?
4 What does the man offer to show them?

3 **Choose a word. Describe it for your partner to guess.**

> You press it to turn on a machine.

> Is it … ?

1 Look at some of Professor Potts' ideas and match them with the sentences.

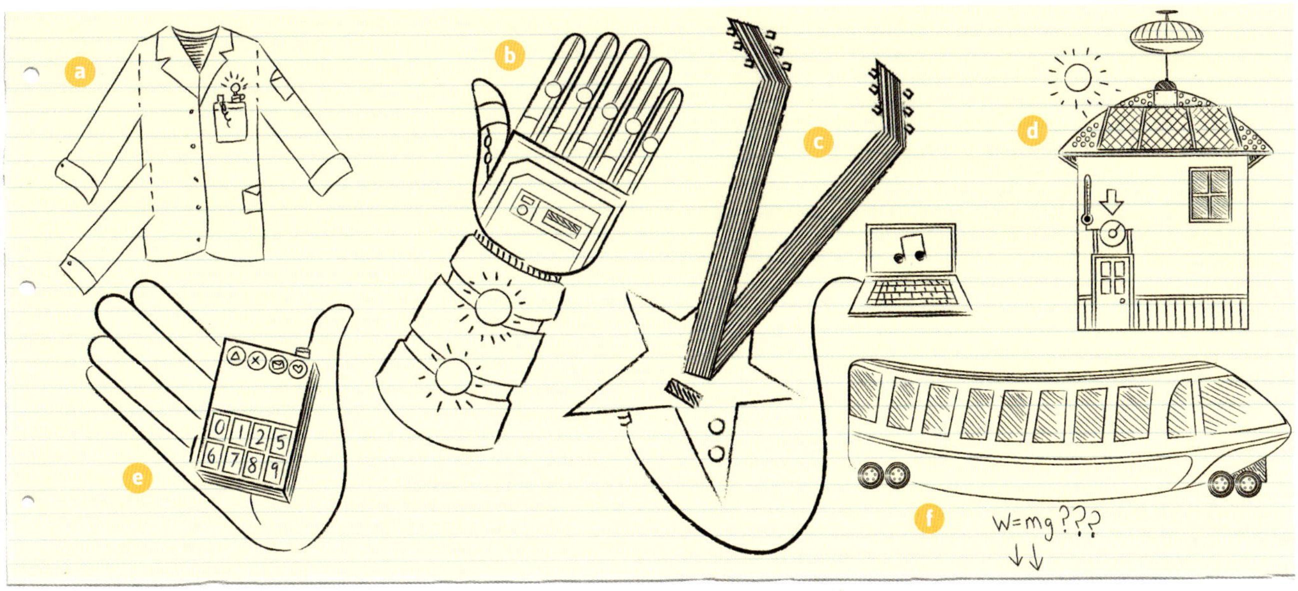

1 It's got too many strings. ☐
2 It's got too many arms. ☐
3 It hasn't got enough wheels. ☐
4 It's got too many fingers. ☐
5 It hasn't got enough windows. ☐
6 It hasn't got enough numbers. ☐

2 068 Watch, listen and say.

Language focus

I've got **too many** jobs to do.
I have**n't** got **enough** time.
I think I need to go and see
A very good friend of mine!

It's got **too many** buttons
And **not enough** power.
To clean this mess, it's going to take
A lot more than an hour.

3 Play *What's wrong?*

1 

2 

3 

4 

5 

6 

7 

8 

9 

10 

11 

12 

It hasn't got enough wheels.

That's picture 4, the go-kart.

1 **Look at the picture. What do you think Lucy is doing?**

2 069 **Read and listen to the dialogue. Check your answers.**

Fred What are you doing, Lucy?
Lucy I'm making a machine.
Fred A machine? Why?
Lucy Because I like inventing things. It's my hobby.
Fred Really? I didn't know that.
Lucy That's because you never asked me before.
Fred So what's the machine for?
Lucy I'm sorry, but I can't tell you.
Fred Why not?
Lucy The reason is that I haven't got enough time to explain. It's a very complicated machine.
Fred It doesn't look too complicated.
Lucy But it's what's inside that's important.
Fred Well, what's inside?
Lucy Something very difficult to understand. That's why I'm not going to tell you.
Fred Fine. I don't really want to know. I'm going. I've got better things to do than waste my time here. Goodbye!
Lucy And there he goes. It works! The 'getting rid of an annoying brother' machine really works.

3 **Practise the dialogue in pairs.**

4 **Work in pairs to make your own dialogue.**

1. With a friend, think of a machine that you'd like to make.
2. Describe why this machine is useful.
3. Make a short dialogue about your machine.
4. Act out your dialogue to the class.

What to say

Giving reasons
Because …
That's because …
The reason is that …
That's why …

1 Read the dialogue and complete the labels on the machine. What do you think the button is for?

Girl Excuse me. Can you tell me what this machine is?

Professor Certainly. It's a weather machine. I use it to control the weather.

Girl Wow! That's so cool. Can you make rain?

Professor Yes, I can. And I can make sunshine too.

Girl Can you tell me what this lever does?

Professor That lever controls the temperature. If you push it up, it gets hotter.

Girl That's amazing. And what about this switch? Can you tell me what this switch is for?

Professor That switch there? It's for starting the wind machine.

Girl Wow! And can you tell me what this button is for?

Professor No, I'm sorry. I can't. That button is top secret!

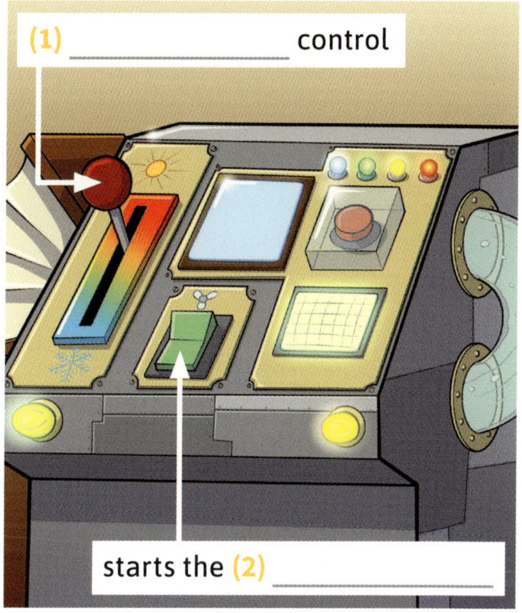

2 Put the words in the correct order.

1 thing / tell / Can / what / me / this / is / ? / you ______________

2 button / Can / tell / what / does / ? / this / you / me ______________

3 for / ? / you / Can / lever / me / what / tell / this / is ______________

3 070 Watch, listen and say.

Language focus

Can you tell me **what** the machine **is**?

Can you tell me **what** this button **does**?

Can you tell me **what** the machine **is for**?

4 Work with a partner. Ask and answer.

Can you tell me what this switch does?

It turns on the train.

PROFESSOR POTTS

1 **Go through the story quickly and find answers to the questions.**

1 How many machines does the professor show them?

2 Is Professor Potts a good inventor?

2 071 **Read and listen to the story to check your answers.**

The professor showed them a strange-looking machine. 'This is my painting machine,' he said. 'You choose something to paint and then you type the word and the colours into the keyboard here at the top.' 'Wow! Can we see it painting something?' asked Phoebe excitedly. 'Certainly,' said the professor. 'I know, let's paint this chair. What colours shall we paint it?' 'Red and yellow,' said Phoebe. 'And would you like spots or stripes?' asked the professor. 'Really? Can we do that?' asked Phoebe. 'Of course,' replied the professor. 'In that case, let's have spots, please!' laughed Phoebe. 'No problem!' said the professor. He went over to the machine and typed at the keyboard, then he pushed a switch and the machine made a strange noise. A big wheel with paintbrushes on it started turning around. A few seconds later, the cat, but *not* the chair, was covered in green and blue spots. 'Oh dear,' said the professor, 'maybe I didn't give it enough time.'

'Can you tell me what this machine does, Professor?' asked Patrick. 'Ah, you'll love my Homework Express! This machine does homework for you – any subject you want.' 'Can we choose Maths?' asked Alex. 'I hate Maths.' 'Certainly,' said the professor proudly. 'What question do you want to ask?' Alex thought and said, 'What's 2,345 x 4,567?' The professor typed in the sum and some coloured lights flashed on the machine. They all looked at the screen. 'I don't think that's right,' said Phoebe. 'Maybe we gave it too many numbers, Professor?'

'This invention is very exciting,' the professor said, showing the children another machine. 'It's a tele-transporter. You put an object in this machine here, press a button and then it travels to that machine over there,' he said, pointing to the opposite corner. 'Let me show you with my bike.' He put his bike inside the machine and pressed a button. Black smoke filled the room. The children and the professor ran over to the other machine and opened the door. 'Oh dear,' said the professor. 'That wasn't supposed to happen. I'll need to get my spanner out.'

'What's this?' asked Phoebe, looking at a machine that looked like a big egg. 'That's my amazing hairdressing machine,' said the professor. 'Choose any style or colour, then sit under it and in five seconds the machine will do your hair for you. Give it a go. You'll love it!'
'Erm, no thanks,' answered Phoebe. 'I like my hair the way it is.'

'Hey, Professor? What happens if I pull this?' asked Patrick, who was standing next to another invention. 'Don't touch that!' shouted the professor. 'That machine isn't finished yet.' Too late! The lever was already down. A yellow light started glowing by the machine. 'Now that's strange,' said the professor. 'I've no idea what that is.'
'But we know what it is,' said Phoebe. 'Goodbye, Professor.' The children walked into the light. They were gone in a flash.

3 **Look at the pictures and answer the questions.**

1 

2 

3 

4 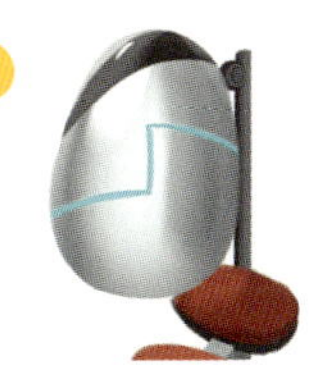

5 

1 What goes wrong with this?
2 What goes wrong with this?
3 What goes wrong with this?
4 Why doesn't Phoebe want to use this?
5 Who pulls this lever?

4 **Think of two new solutions for each of the professor's problems.**

1 He wants to paint a chair.
2 He wants to do Alex's Math's homework.
3 He wants to move a bike.
4 He wants to cut Phoebe's hair.

He can teach his cat to paint.

That's funny!

He can paint the chair with a paintbrush.

That's a great idea!

1 Work in pairs. Look at the five inventions in the photos. Number them 1–5 (1 = the earliest invention). Which two were invented around the same time?

2 Read the webpage to check your answers.

The five greatest inventions of the 20th century

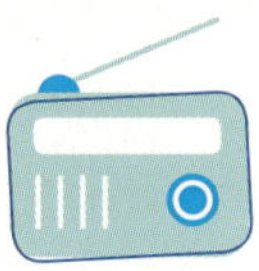

What? The radio

Why? The radio is the most important and the oldest of these inventions. Most people think that Guglielmo Marconi invented the radio. In 1901, he sent the first radio message from England to Canada. His invention made it easier for people around the world to communicate.

What? The plane

Why? Some people say that the American Wright brothers invented the plane in 1903. Other people think that the Brazilian Santos-Dumont invented it at around the same time. The plane has made travelling around the world much quicker and easier.

What? The television

Why? Can you imagine your life without TV? Watching TV is the favourite hobby of many children and adults all over the world. It was in 1926 that John Logie Baird demonstrated how moving objects could be televised. However, today there are many families in the world who haven't got a TV.

What? The computer

Why? It's impossible to say when the computer was invented, but many people agree that Steve Jobs and Steve Wozniak first brought the computer into people's homes. The computer they introduced in 1977 is very different to the ones that we use today. Computers have changed the way that we live and work.

What? The mobile phone

Why? Before the invention of the mobile phone in the 1970s, people made phone calls to houses (using what we now call 'landlines'). If the person who you wanted to talk to wasn't at home, bad luck! The mobile phone has made communication much easier, and today more than half of the world owns a mobile phone.

3 Discuss in pairs.

1 Which is the most important invention on the list? Why?
2 Think of two more inventions that could be on the list and say why.

1 **Work in pairs. Look at the strange inventions and try to decide what they are for.**

I think it's a …

Maybe it's for …

I've no idea.

1

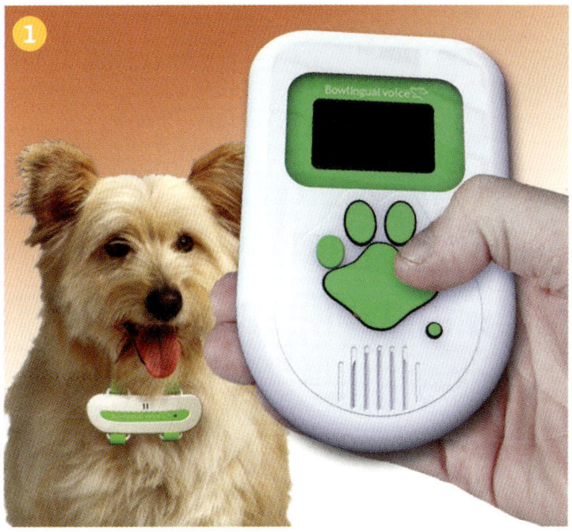

2

3

4

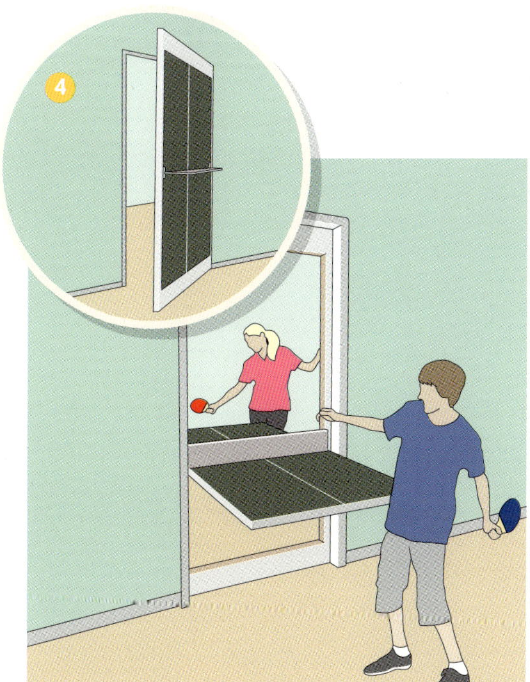

2 072 **Listen to a radio show about the inventions and check your ideas.**

3 **Work in pairs. Discuss together.**

a Take turns to explain what each of the inventions does.

b Decide on a mark to give each invention.

0 = useless	2 = quite a good idea
1 = a bit silly	3 = brilliant

4 **Work in pairs. Design a crazy invention.**

a Think of something that you do every day which you don't like doing or find difficult.

b Think how you can make this easier.

c Think of a machine (or other invention) to help you.

d Draw a picture of your machine and give it a name.

Simple machines

Super fact!

People first used wheels to make pots 7,000 years ago. 2,000 years later, they put wheels on carts!

What kinds of machines are there?

1 073 Look, listen and number.

Simple machines

lever family

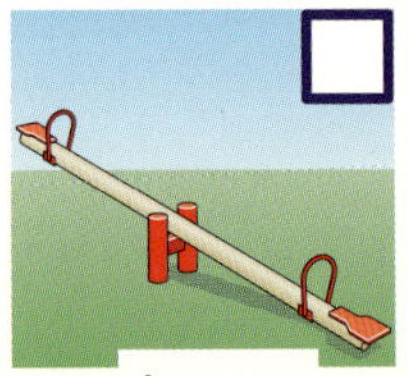

levers

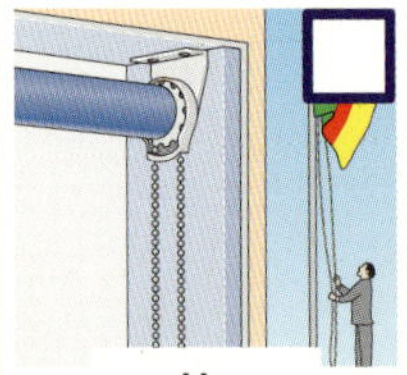

pulleys

wheels and axles

wedge family

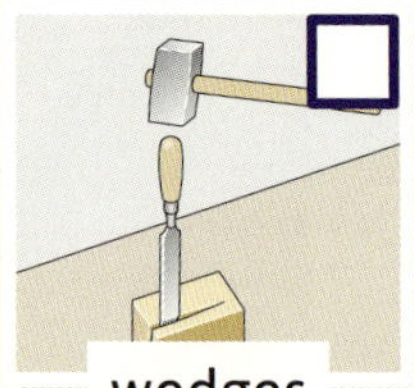

wedges

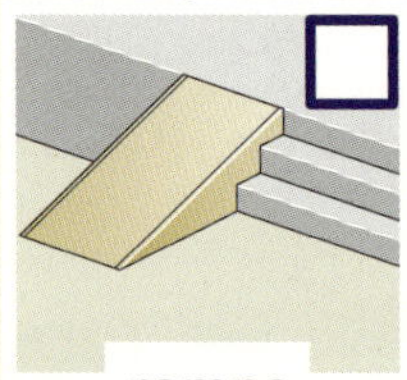

ramps

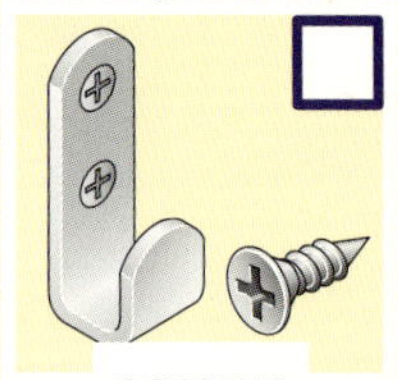

screws

2 Work in pairs. Read and answer. Which simple machines help us to:

1 move wheelchairs up and down?
2 lift things that are difficult to move?
3 move a flag up and down?
4 put something on a wall?
5 move heavy things?
6 move things apart quickly?

Simple machines help us to move things.

Levers help us to lift things that are difficult to move. A seesaw is a lever. Kids can play on a seesaw at the playground. Bottle openers are also levers. They help us to lift the top off a bottle.

A pulley helps us to lift things up or down. A pulley is a rope that sits on a wheel. You pull on the rope to move things. Pulleys help us to move a flag up and down.

Wheels and axles help us to move heavy things. The axle sits in the centre of the wheel. The wheel turns around the axle. Cars use four wheels and axles. Big wheels in funfairs are made of a very large wheel and axle.

Wedges help us to move things apart quickly or to stop them moving. Knives and axes are examples of wedges. A door wedge keeps a door from closing.

We use **ramps** to move heavy things from one place to another. There are ramps outside some shops. Ramps help people in wheelchairs to move up and down.

Screws are also a type of wedge. We use them to join things together, like pieces of wood or metal. We use screws to make furniture or to put mirrors on walls.

3 Look at the wheelbarrow and find the simple machines that move it. Then read and answer: What's a *compound machine*?

A wheelbarrow is a compound machine. A compound machine is made from different simple machines. The wheelbarrow is made from three different simple machines:

- The wheel and axle make the wheelbarrow move. They help you move heavy things in the wheelbarrow.
- The handles are levers. They help you lift heavy things in the wheelbarrow.
- There are screws that join the handles to the wheelbarrow.

4 Look at the two compound machines and write the words on the diagrams. You can use some words more than once.

lever wedge screw wheel and axle

1

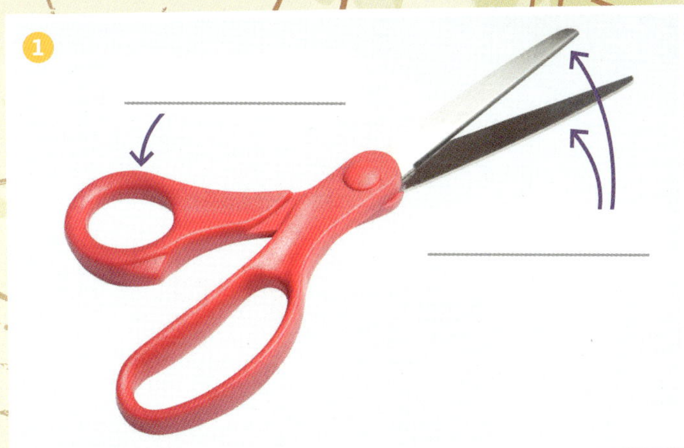

2

5 Work in pairs. Look around the classroom and find a simple machine and a compound machine. Explain how they work.

- Can you see a lever?
- Does it have a wedge?
- Is there a screw?
- What does it do?
- How does it work?

6 Project Draw a toy to put in a park for younger children. Label the parts. Explain how the toy works.

- What type of toy is it?
- What does it do?
- How does it help children?

Draw your machine and tell the class about it.

Get talking

Building a treehouse

1 Work in pairs. Choose a role card.

Student A

You want to build a treehouse.

You ask your older brother/sister for information. Think about:

- the materials that you need
- the tools that you need
- a good place to build it
- how long it will take
- what help you're going to need

Student B

You are helping to plan a treehouse.

Help your younger brother/sister plan his/her treehouse. Think about:

- what materials he/she needs
- what sort of tools he/she needs
- a good place to build it
- how long it will take him/her
- what jobs you can do to help

2 Act out your dialogue.

Student A

I'd like to …

Do I need … ?

What sort of tools … ?

I don't think I can …

Could you do that for me?

Student B

First of all, you need …

The tools you need are …

Maybe you also need …

Why not build it in the big tree which is … ?

I could … for you, but let's ask Mum/Dad to …

Think and write

A story

1 Read the two stories. Which one is better: Ethan's or Sophie's?

Yesterday I visited Professor Madly in her lab. She showed me a machine. I wanted to know what the machine did. I asked the professor. The professor told me. It was an ice-cream machine. I asked for some strawberry ice cream. The professor didn't have enough strawberries at home. Then she pressed two buttons. The machine made some ice cream for me. It was very nice.
Ethan, 6A

Yesterday I visited Professor Madly in her lab. She showed me a strange-looking machine. It looked like a laptop, but it had wheels and lots of colourful buttons. I was curious. 'Can you tell me what this machine does?' I asked the professor. She smiled. 'This machine can make the best ice cream in the world!' 'Wow! Can you please make me some strawberry ice cream?' I asked.
The professor shook her head and answered, 'I'm sorry. We haven't got enough strawberries at home.'
Then she pressed the yellow button and the brown button. 'Here you are,' she said. I was so happy. The ice cream was fantastic – vanilla and chocolate.
Sophie, 6A

2 Underline the adjectives which Sophie uses.
Then make a list of other adjectives.

3 How many times do the professor and Sophie speak in her story?

4 Use adjectives and direct speech to make this story better.

When I went home, the professor gave me a box. At home I opened it. There was a machine in it. I wanted to know what the machine did. I phoned the professor. The professor told me. It was a weather machine. I asked for some sunshine. The professor told me to press the yellow button on the machine. It started to rain. The professor wasn't happy. It was a mistake.

Writing tip

You can make a story sound more lively if you use direct speech. Adjectives also make your story more interesting.

5 Imagine that you visited the professor last night.
Write your story.

7 This is Houston

1 074 **Listen and say the words. Check with your partner.**

1969 was an exciting year in the history of space travel. American Neil Armstrong and his colleague Edwin Aldrin were the first people to land on the moon. They took photos, collected stones and left a message. It said: 'Here men from the planet Earth first set foot upon the moon July 1969, AD. We came in peace for all mankind.' Armstrong and Aldrin only stayed for two and a half hours before they left the moon again in the Eagle Lunar Module.

1 countdown clock
2 lunar module
3 space capsule
4 spacesuit
5 launch pad
6 crater
7 control panel
8 headset
9 screen

BIG QUESTION What do we know about space?

2 075 **Read, listen and complete the sentences.**

1 The three friends find themselves in a kind of ________________.
2 It is the year ________________ and on the screen they can see ________________.
3 An engineer asks them what they ________________.
4 He tells security to ________________.

3 **Choose a word. Describe it for your partner to guess.**

You use this to listen to people talking.

I know. It's a …

1 Read and match the speech bubbles with the pictures.

1. Floating in the air is fun. ☐
2. Flying to the moon is exciting. ☐
3. Eating in the capsule needs practice. ☐
4. Exercising is very important. ☐
5. Putting on a spacesuit takes longer than clothes. ☐
6. Sleeping in the capsule is uncomfortable. ☐
7. Being away from your family is difficult. ☐
8. Looking at Earth from space is wonderful. ☐

a

b

c

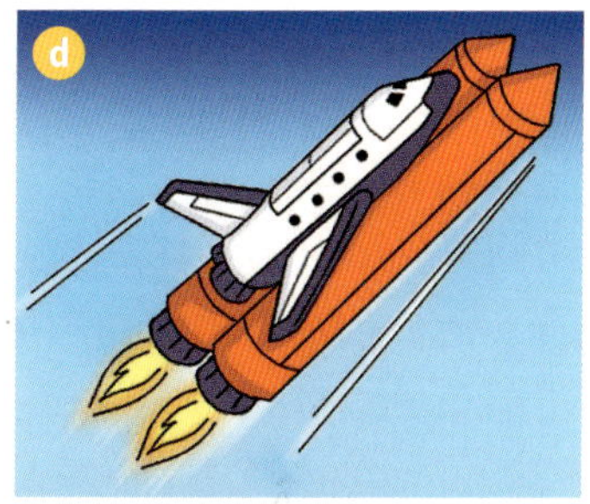
d

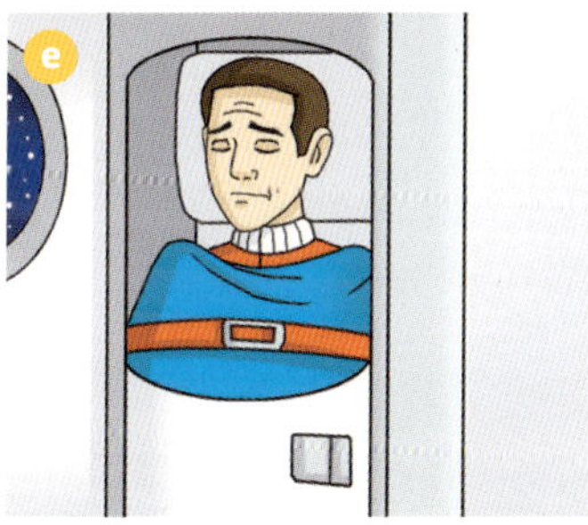
e

f

g

h

2 076 Watch, listen and say.

Language focus

Going on a space trip is exciting!
Looking at the sky is such fun!
Staying up late is really tiring.
I need to go to bed – it's almost one!

3 Work in groups. Discuss things that you do at school or at home. Which of these things are boring / interesting / important / fun? Do you all agree?

Helping at home is boring.

It depends. I don't mind cooking.

Having friends at your house is fun.

Definitely!

Studying for a test is important.

I agree, but it's boring too!

1 077 **Listen and answer the questions. Then sing the song.**

1 Is Commander Graham an astronaut or an engineer?
2 What can the astronaut see from the window?
3 What do you think happens at the end?

Commander Graham, this is Ground Control.
Can you hear us where you are?
It's Commander Graham. Hello, Ground Control.
Things are going well so far!

Looking down from here is wonderful.
Flying fast through space is fun,
So is looking at the Earth, oh yeah,
In the golden morning sun!

Commander Graham ...

Watching the stars come up is nice.
Oh, my trip is just so great!
Now I really need to go to bed.
I'm so sorry, it's getting late.

Commander Graham, this is Ground Control.
Can you hear us where you are?

All about music:
ELECTRONIC MUSIC

Back in the 1970s, a German band called Kraftwerk started doing something that no other band was doing. They didn't use guitars or drums. They used electronic sounds and computers to make music. This new 'electronic' music became very popular in the 1980s and these days many bands use computers to write their music.

What I think about this song

It's great. It's OK. I don't really like it.

Phonics

2 079 **Listen and say the dialogue.**

Gus Hi, Mum. It's Gus. What's up?

Mum Well, I've just had some lovely plums covered in honey for lunch. How are you, son?

Gus Um ... hungry!

1 Read the interview with an alien. The journalist lost her notes before she wrote her newspaper report. Correct five mistakes in the report.

Journalist	What's your name?
Alien	I'm Zonrak.
Journalist	Where are you from?
Alien	I'm from the planet Alpha 346.
Journalist	How old are you?
Alien	I'm three hundred and thirty-seven years old.
Journalist	What's your favourite food?
Alien	Grass with vanilla sauce.
Journalist	Really?
Alien	And I like chocolate soup.
Journalist	How many languages do you speak?
Alien	A hundred and thirty-three.
Journalist	Wow! Thank you very much!

ALIEN

SEEN IN OUR TOWN

Yesterday morning I spoke to an alien who landed his space capsule in the middle of our town. The alien said that he was from Mars and that he was 327 years old. He said that his favourite food was spaghetti with vanilla sauce. He also said that he liked strawberry soup. The alien said that he spoke 339 languages!

2 Complete these sentences using reported speech.

1 I am from the moon. ➜ The alien said that ______________________.

2 I like chocolate soup. ➜ The alien said that ______________________.

3 080 Watch, listen and say.

Language focus

I met an astronaut today.
He **said that he was** back from the stars.
He **said that he liked** our planet best.
But he **said that he had to** visit Mars.

He **said that he didn't know** the way.
He **said that he wanted** a map.
But I **said that I didn't have** one.
And that's because I'm a cat.

4 Read the newspaper report about the interview with the alien's wife. Complete the interview.

ALIEN'S WIFE

NOW HERE TOO!

Yesterday evening our journalist spoke to the alien's wife. She said that she was 412 years old and that her name was Funflower.

Journalist	How (1) ______________________?
Alien's wife	I'm (2) ______________________.
Journalist	What (3) ______________________?
Alien's wife	(4) ______________________.

5 Read the rest of the interview and complete the report.

Journalist	What's your favourite food?
Alien's wife	My favourite food is cornflakes with broccoli.
Journalist	What do you like to drink?
Alien's wife	I like insect juice.
Journalist	How many languages do you speak?
Alien's wife	I speak 162.

She said that her favourite food (1) ______________________.
She said that she (2) ______________________ insect juice.
The alien's wife also said that she (3) ______________________ languages!

ALEX, THE **ENGINEER**

1 **Go through the story quickly and find answers to the questions.**

1 Why do you think the engineers are sleeping?

2 Why do you think Alex is at the control panel?

2 081 **Read and listen to the story to check your answers.**

The children were scared. They weren't spies, but they couldn't explain anything. 'Come with me!' said the security officer. At that moment, the engineer who was standing next to him suddenly said, 'I'm feeling … dizzy.' He sat down and a minute later he was asleep. Then the security officer sat down and he too fell asleep.

'How strange!' Alex thought. He looked around and saw that all the engineers were sleeping at their computers and the security officers were asleep too. 'Maybe they're all tired,' Patrick said. 'Come on. Now's our chance! Let's go!' 'No,' said Alex, 'there's something strange going on!' 'I've got it!' said Phoebe. 'They were all drinking tea when they fell asleep. There was something in their tea!' 'Maybe the engineer was right,' Alex said. 'He said that this room was top secret. Perhaps there *are* spies who want the mission to fail!' 'Hello, Houston?' They suddenly heard a voice coming through the headsets that were lying on the desk. 'This is Neil speaking. Anyone there? We need your help up here!' Phoebe was very excited. 'Listen! That's Neil Armstrong! We must help him!'

A few minutes later, they were sitting at a computer wearing headsets and Alex was working at the control panel. 'Houston, we're going back to the space capsule!' 'What's your temperature?' asked Alex. '370° Celsius!' the voice replied. 'Uh-oh, that's too high,' Alex said. 'Try cooling the engines a bit!' 'Thanks, Houston. Cooling the engines right now!'

Alex was doing really well, talking to them like an engineer and giving them instructions. Half an hour later, the astronauts left the moon and were on their way to the space capsule.

'Hey, what's going on here?' asked one of the engineers, waking up. 'I'm talking to Neil Armstrong. They're on their way back to Earth!' Alex replied. 'You're … what?' asked the engineer. 'Give me a headset!' he said angrily, so Phoebe quickly gave him hers. As the engineer put it on, he heard Neil Armstrong again. 'Everything's perfect up here. Our new colleague down there's really cool. Congratulations, Houston! Where on *Earth* did you find him?'

Alex smiled at the engineer and took off his headset. They looked around and saw that all the other engineers were sitting at their computers again. Everything looked normal.

'I'm sorry, kids. We found the spy. It was one of our own engineers. And now you've saved the day!' one of the security officers said. 'No problem. I was happy to help,' said Alex. 'But how did you know what to do?' 'I've got Moonlanding 2000 at home. I learnt everything from that. I love it!' Alex replied. 'Moonlanding 2000? What's that?' the engineer asked. 'It's a computer moon flight simulation game! I'm really good at it,' Alex explained. 'I've got no idea what you're talking about, but you're good!' the engineer laughed.

The engineer was still confused when the children saw the yellow light glowing. They stepped into it. They were gone in a flash.

3 Put the sentences in order.

- Neil Armstrong asked the control room for help. ☐
- They didn't understand how Alex helped to save the mission. ☐
- Phoebe, Alex and Patrick were in a space control room. ☐
- The children put on headsets and Alex spoke to the astronauts. ☐
- When the engineers woke up, they were very surprised. ☐
- Suddenly all the people in the room fell asleep. ☐
- Phoebe thought that there was something strange in their tea. ☐
- His instructions helped them to return to the space capsule. ☐

4 Play *Delete the text*. Your teacher will write this text on the board. Ask questions about the text. Your teacher will delete any words from the text that are in the answers.

The three Time Travellers were in the control room in Houston. On a big screen on the wall they saw the first landing on the moon, so they were very excited. All the engineers and security officers fell asleep because there was something in their tea.

How many Time Travellers are there?

What did they … ?

Where were … ?

1 082 **When do you think these things happened? Match the dates and the photos. Then listen and check.**

1 12th April 1961   2 20th July 1969   3 16th June 1963   4 28th April 2001

a

First space tourist

b

First woman in space

c

First man in space

d

First person on the moon

2 083 **Listen again and answer the questions.**

1 How long did Yuri Gagarin spend in space?
2 Who was Valentina Tereshkova?
3 What was the name of Neil Armstrong's space ship?
4 How far did Neil Armstrong travel from Earth to the moon?
5 How much did Dennis Tito pay for his space trip?
6 How long did Dennis Tito train for his journey?

3 **Complete the competition entry.**

Do you want a free journey into space? Tell us in no more than 50 words why we should take you. The best answer wins a place on the next trip to Mars.

Name: ______________________________

Age: ______________________________

I want to go into space because

____

____

____

____

4 **Work in small groups. Interview each other for the competition in Activity 3. Decide who wins the trip from your group.**

1 Look at the pictures and the headings. What do you think happens in the story?

PART 1: LOST IN SPACE

It was 1957. At the US space centre, scientists were getting two monkeys ready for a journey into space. The scientists chose the two most intelligent monkeys, a male and a female. They called them Leo and Rosy. The scientists put the monkeys into the space capsule and said goodbye.

The spaceship took off. In the control room, the scientists could hear the noises that the monkeys made. For two and a half days there were no problems. Then, on the third day, they lost contact with the space capsule forever. Leo and Rosy were lost in space …

PART 2: THE PLANET OF THE MONKEYS

It was 2757. The excited scientists of COSPACE were sitting in front of the screen of the control room. COSPACE was an international space programme. Today was their first ever landing on the planet Pluto.

'Control. We're 3,000 metres above the planet … we're going down.' In their headsets the scientists heard the voice of Matt Cormack from the spaceship.

'Two hundred … a hundred … we have landed!'

The astronauts opened the door of their space capsule. There were hundreds of 'people' outside. But were they people? No, they were monkeys!

The chief of the monkeys spoke into a microphone.

'Welcome to our planet!' he said.

PART 3: A NEW BEGINNING

Cormack asked the chief about the history of his people. 'We don't know everything,' he said 'but I can take you somewhere you might find answers!'

They went to a huge museum. Outside was a golden statue of two monkeys. Cormack knew immediately who they were – Leo and Rosy!

A day later, Commander Cormack stood before all the monkeys. 'We want to say sorry. Many years ago we did terrible things to animals. Today, animals are our friends, and we share the Earth with them. We look forward to a great friendship with you forever.'

2 084 Read and listen to the story. Answer the questions.

1 Why did the scientists choose Leo and Rosy?
2 When did the scientists lose contact with the monkeys?
3 What did Cormack find on Pluto?
4 What was the first thing the chief said to Cormack?
5 Where did the chief take Cormack?
6 Why did Cormack say sorry?

3 Discuss the questions in pairs.

1 What do you think the chief did next?
2 What do you think Commander Cormack did next?

SPACE

What are stars?

Super fact!

Before Apollo went to the moon, the astronauts learned the shapes of the constellations. They wanted to know how to find the way back to Earth if their computers stopped working.

1 085 **Look, listen and number.**

the solar system

galaxy

gas

burn

2 What do you know about stars? Read the sentences. Write *t* (true) or *f* (false).

1 Stars are spheres made of gas. ☐

2 Stars are smaller than planets. ☐

3 The Sun is the closest star to Earth. ☐

4 There are about 10 billion stars in our galaxy. ☐

5 Stars burn for millions of years. ☐

3 Now read about stars and check your answers.

STAR★FACTORY

When we look at the night sky, we can often see stars. Stars are very big, burning spheres of gas. They look small to us, but they're bigger than planets. The Sun is a star. It's at the centre of our solar system and is the closest star to Earth.

Stars start in big, cold clouds of gas called star factories. These clouds break up and get very, very hot, and then a star is created. Stars take millions of years to burn all the gas inside them. Then we can't see them anymore.

A group of stars is called a galaxy. Our galaxy is called the Milky Way and it has more than 100 billion stars in it. It's called the Milky Way because people think that it looks like a road made of milk.

4 Complete the three questions to match the answers. Use the information from the text.

1 What ____________________? They are huge spheres of gas.

2 Where ____________________? In big cold clouds of gas.

3 Why ____________________? Because it looks like a road of milk.

5 Read and answer. What is a constellation? Now write the missing words.

stories constellations billions sky

A constellation is a group of stars that makes a shape in the night (1) ______________. When you look at a constellation, the stars look close to each other but they are (2) ______________ of kilometres away from each other.
There are many (3) ______________ in the Milky Way. Some of them have the names of characters from (4) ______________, like *Orion*. Others are named after things because they look like them.

Orion

Big Bear

Little Bear

6 Read about a constellation. What is it called and why?

LEO (THE LION)

What constellations are near it?
Cancer and Coma Berenices

Why is it called Leo?
Leo means *lion*. It's named after a lion from a Greek story. The lion had gold fur and arrows could not go through it.

7 **Project** Find out about a constellation. Draw it and write its name in English. Answer the questions about it.

- What is it called and why?
- Name two constellations that are next to it.
- What does it look like?
- Is there a story about the constellation?

Get talking

A class survey on television

1 086 **Listen to a discussion and number the types of TV programmes.**

films	☐	comedies	☐
documentaries	☐	the news	☐
cartoons	☐	police dramas	☐
reality TV shows	☐	soaps	☐
sports programmes	☐	game shows	☐

2 **Complete a class survey about television.**

Think about it

- In class, collect ideas about television programmes.
  - What is the most important event that you have ever seen on TV?
  - What is your favourite programme?
  - Is there a television programme which you don't like at all?
  - What programme do you watch every day?
  - What programme do you watch every week?
  - Have you got a TV in your bedroom?
  - How many hours do you watch TV per day from Monday to Friday?
  - How many hours do you watch TV per day at the weekend?

Prepare it

- Divide into eight groups. Each group takes one question and asks everyone in the class.
- Make a note of the names to make sure that your group has only asked each person once.

Present it

- Work in groups. Use your notes to prepare a large bar chart like the one on the right.
- Each group shows their bar chart to the class and explains it.

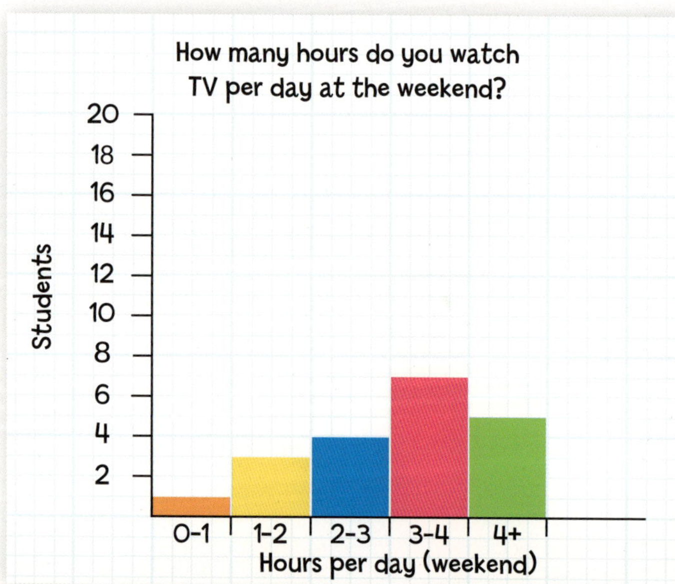

Presenting tip

Make a big bar chart and write the numbers clearly so that your classmates can see them. Colour the bars in different colours that you can say in English. Make sure that you talk about the colour when you point to the chart.

Think and write

A post on a discussion forum

1 Read the posts on a discussion forum. Do the writers all agree?

SPEAK OUT Animals in space

AUTHOR	THREAD: ANIMALS IN SPACE
happyface	I think it's terrible that they have sent monkeys into space and that many of them have never come back. Poor animals!
Anja12	My favourite animals are cats. I felt sad when I heard about a cat in a rocket. It's horrible for a cat to be in a rocket.
onlyme	Please help to stop space travel experiments with animals. They want to live a happy life!
thethinker	All experiments with animals are wrong. Animals have rights too!

2 Here are ideas from other posts on the forum. Match the sentence halves.

1 Sending animals into space
2 I feel sorry for
3 I can't believe that
4 Humans shouldn't

a send animals into space.
b they sent animals into space.
c is awful.
d those poor animals.

3 Write posts for these discussion threads on 'Speak out'. Say what you think.

SPEAK OUT Cutting down the rainforest

SPEAK OUT Testing medicine on animals

Writing tip

An Internet forum is for expressing your feelings. These phrases help you to say what you think and feel.
I think … should / shouldn't …
It's not a good idea / a good idea to …
Please don't …
I think it's sad (wrong / good / a great idea) when …
I felt (sad / sorry) when I heard that …

8 A cold place

At the North Pole, the summer days are very long and in winter it's dark for six months. On 21st December, the sun doesn't rise, so it's dark all day. In winter you can sometimes see the Northern Lights there. This is an amazing show of colours which light up the sky. People used to believe that these Northern Lights were the flames of dragons flying across the sky. This Arctic land of the midnight sun is the home of about 4 million people. Today, they live in modern homes, not in igloos or tents.

1 087 **Listen and say the words. Check with your partner.**

1 Northern Lights
2 iceberg
3 polar bear
4 polar bear cub
5 ice floe
6 seal
7 seal pup
8 igloo
9 mittens
10 sledge

BIG QUESTION What's it like at the Earth's poles?

2 088 **Read, listen and answer the questions.**

1 Where are Patrick's mittens?
2 What are Patrick and Alex doing?
3 Who built the snowman?
4 What is Phoebe looking at?

3 **Choose a word for your partner to spell.**

1 **Read the dialogue and answer the questions.**

Grace My grandparents are going to the Arctic for a holiday. They've always wanted to see the aurora borealis.

Jack The aurora borealis? They're the Northern Lights, aren't they?

Grace That's right. Aurora borealis is the scientific name for them.

Jack So how are they getting there?

Grace By ship. They're taking a cruise to the north of Norway.

Jack That's the best place to see the lights, isn't it?

Grace One of them. You can sometimes see them in the UK, in Scotland.

Jack But Scotland isn't as good, is it?

Grace I think Norway is better because it's nearer the North Pole.

1 Where are Grace's grandparents going?
2 What is the aurora borealis?
3 Why is Norway a good place to see the lights?

2 **Complete the sentences using *is it*, *isn't it*, *are they* or *aren't they*.**

1 The North Pole is in the Arctic, ______________?
2 The Northern Lights aren't at the South Pole, ______________?
3 Scotland isn't in the Arctic, ______________?
4 You grandparents are lucky, ______________?

3 089 **Watch, listen and say.**

Language focus

It's cold at the poles, **isn't it**?
And the nights are dark, **aren't they**?
Great for a polar bear perhaps,
But not a good place for me.

There isn't much sun there, **is there**?
The days aren't long, **are they**?
A good place for penguins perhaps,
But I'd better stay away.

4 **Work in pairs. Take it in turns to guess and answer about your favourite TV programme, food, game, animals or other ideas.**

1 Look at the quiz. Answer the questions with a partner.

How much do you know about penguins?

1. **Penguins live at the …**
   a) North Pole. b) South Pole.
2. **Penguins are …**
   a) fish.
   b) birds.
3. **Penguins …**
   a) can fly.
   b) can't fly.

2 090 Read and listen to the dialogue. Check your answers.

Daisy Ben, can I check something, please? Is the Geography homework for tomorrow?
Ben That's right.
Daisy And just remind me. It's about the North Pole, isn't it?
Ben No, you've got that wrong. It's about the South Pole.
Daisy Oh well! It's lucky that I haven't started it yet.
Ben You've got to choose an animal that lives there and write about it.
Daisy Did you say 'animal'?
Ben Yes, any animal you want.
Daisy So I can't write about penguins, can I?
Ben Why not?
Daisy Well, because penguins aren't animals, are they?
Ben Why aren't they animals? I think you're confused.
Daisy They're fish, aren't they?
Ben What! Penguins aren't fish. They're birds.
Daisy But they can't fly, can they?
Ben No, they can't. But they are birds. And anyway, birds and fish are animals too. I think you need to go and do some research.

3 Practise the dialogue in pairs.

4 Work in pairs to make your own dialogue.

1 With a friend, list the homework you've got this week.
2 Think of some questions to check information about the homework.
3 Make a short dialogue about the homework.
4 Act out your dialogue to the class.

What to say

Checking information
… are they?
… isn't it?
Just remind me …
Can I just check something, please?
Did you say … ?

1 Read the magazine interview with a scientist and complete it with the questions from the box.

What does it mean for the animals? | Is that right? | What can we do about this?

Interviewer Some scientists think that the Arctic might be in danger. (1) ______________________?

Scientist Yes, it is. Most scientists think this.

Interviewer What might happen?

Scientist Well, the climate is getting warmer and the ice may melt.

Interviewer (2) ______________________?

Scientist If the ice melts, the animals in the region may find life very difficult. They will have to swim a long way to find food, so some species, like the polar bear for example, might become very rare.

Interviewer (3) ______________________?

Scientist Well, the first thing we can do is take the problem seriously. We should let our politicians know that we are worried.

2 Replace a word in each sentence with the word or words in brackets.

1 The Arctic is in danger. (might be)
2 The ice melts. (may melt)
3 The polar bear will become very rare. (might)
4 If we don't act now, it will be too late. (may)

3 091 Watch, listen and say.

Language focus

The jungle **may** be in danger
Because people want our trees.
They **might** take our home away.
Don't let this happen, please.

The Arctic **may** be in trouble.
The ice is melting fast.
Polar bears won't find food.
There **might** not be enough to last.

4 Work in groups. Play the game.

Picture 1 may be a …

I don't think so. It might be a …

RESCUING THE SEAL PUPS

1 **Go through the story quickly and find answers to the questions.**

1 How does Phoebe know a lot about seals?
2 What do the men on the ski-doo want?

2 092 **Read and listen to the story to check your answers.**

The three friends took the spades and walked towards the sea. As they came closer to the beach, they could see six seal pups on an ice floe. 'Did you know that they're called whitecoats?' asked Phoebe. 'They don't go into the water for four or five weeks. First, their mothers feed them, but then they go hungry for some time. Their fur changes colour and, after that, they can go into the water to hunt.' 'Did you read all that in a book?' asked Patrick. 'No,' she replied, 'I saw it in a documentary about Canadian seals. And did you know that nobody is allowed to hunt them in Canada? They're protected.' 'OK, know-it-all, but we're not going to hunt them, so let's get closer and then we can see them,' suggested Alex. 'Closer? You're mad!' said Patrick. '*You* may want to get your feet wet, but I certainly don't!' 'We shouldn't get closer anyway,' said Phoebe. 'We might scare them.'

Suddenly they heard the noise of a ski-doo. It stopped at the edge of the beach and two men got off. They were carrying sticks and had big knives in their belts. 'They're going to kill the seal pups for their fur!' said Patrick. 'Sorry, Phoebe, but we *have* to jump on the ice right *now* to save those pups.'

The children jumped onto the ice and the two boys used their spades to push the ice floe out into the sea. The two men tried to jump onto the ice floe, but it was already too far away from the beach, so they fell into the water. They shouted angrily at the children, then went back to their ski-doo and drove away.

'How are we going to get back to the land?' Alex asked. 'Well, we can't swim,' said Phoebe, 'because the water is too cold.'

Half an hour later, they heard a helicopter, so they started to wave. The pilot saw them and lowered a man on a rope to rescue them. When they were safely in the helicopter, the pilot said, 'What were you doing? That was very dangerous. You were lucky that we were out looking for two men and came this way.' 'We saw two men!' exclaimed Alex. They described the men and the pilot radioed the police.

A little later, the helicopter landed at a police station. 'We think that we've found those two men,' one of the police officers said, 'but can you identify them for us, please?' He showed them some photos and the boys pointed to the two men. 'That's them!' said Phoebe.

They left the police station and walked down to the beach to find more seals. There weren't any seals on the beach, but there was a big ice floe with a hole in it. Around the hole was a glowing yellow light. 'Oh no … that water's freezing!' said Patrick … but the children jumped into the hole. They were gone in a flash.

3 **Complete the sentences. You can use 1, 2, 3 or 4 words.**

1. Closer to the beach, the three friends could see seal pups ______________.
2. Seal pups don't go into the water for ______________.
3. Nobody is allowed to hunt ______________.
4. The pilot said that the children were ______________.
5. The police wanted the children to look at ______________.
6. The three friends jumped ______________.

4 **Read and do the puzzle.**

There are lots of seals in our area. Every year the size of the colony of seals doubles, so in 2019 there were 16, and in 2020 there were 32.

When did the first pair of seals arrive?
How many are there now?

1 Discuss in pairs. What differences do you know between the Arctic and the Antarctic?

Is the Arctic where … ?

I don't think … live in the Antarctic.

2 093 Listen to the radio show and check your answers.

3 094 Listen again and write *Arctic* or *Antarctic* under the pictures.

1 

2 

3 

4 

5 

6 

4 Work in pairs. Imagine you are going on an expedition to the South Pole. Make a list of the five most important things you will need.

We'll definitely need … because …

I think we should take … because …

How about …?

We've forgotten … ! That's important because …

5 Discuss with the rest of the class. Agree on a class list.

1 Read the magazine article. Did Scott's dream come true?

Real-life HEROES

Scott of the Antarctic

Captain Robert Falcon Scott, or Scott of the Antarctic as he is often called, was an officer in the Navy. He is famous because he wanted to be the first man to go to the South Pole. In June 1910, he left the UK to travel to the other side of the world.

He started travelling across the ice with sledges and dogs, but the weather was so bad that he sent them back to camp with some of his team. Scott and four other men, Wilson, Oates, Bower and Evans, continued on foot.

The weather was really bad, but on January 17th 1912, the men finally arrived at the South Pole. However, when they arrived, they found a Norwegian flag! They were not the first people to go to the South Pole because the Norwegians arrived a few weeks before them. Now they had a hard 1,500 km journey back to their ship.

The weather was really terrible and in the middle of February, Evans fell and died. A few weeks later, Oates, who knew that he was dying and making the journey too slow for the other men, left the tent. He told the others that he was going for a walk, but he didn't come back.

Scott and the other men carried on, but around March 29th 1912, they all died. They were only 20km from their camp. Their bodies were found eight months later, together with Scott's diary, which told the whole sad story.

2 Read the article again and put the events in the order they happened.

- Scott travels to the Antarctic on a special trip. ☐
- Oates disappears. ☐
- Scott dies. ☐
- Scott's diary is found. ☐
- Scott sends the dogs and sledges back to camp. ☐
- Scott arrives at the South Pole. ☐

3 Work in pairs. Read and talk about heroes.

For many people, Scott was a great hero. A hero is a good person who does something very brave. Make a list of people who you think are heroes. Think about:

- what they did.
- why they are so special.

4 Choose one of your heroes and write about them.

The hero I want to write about is ...
He/She was the ...

The Arctic

What life is there in the Arctic?

Super fact!

Arctic foxes live in burrows underground and they have the warmest fur of all the Arctic animals.

1 095 Look, listen and number.

reindeer

Arctic hare

walrus

Arctic fox

narwhal

moss

2 Read about the Arctic. Write the titles in the left column.

Arctic animals Tundra habitat Arctic seas

Features of the Arctic	What's it like?
1	This is one of the coldest places on Earth. It's difficult for people to live here. The wind is strong and icy and there isn't much rain. In winter, it sometimes snows and the soil is frozen. Small plants, like moss and grass, grow here, but there aren't any trees.
2	Different herbivores and carnivores live in the Arctic. Reindeer and Arctic hares are herbivores. Arctic foxes are carnivores and the biggest carnivores are polar bears. Polar bears hunt seals and other sea creatures.
3	The Arctic Ocean is the smallest ocean. It's so cold in the Arctic that the surface of the ocean freezes and turns into ice. The water below the ice is home to mammals like narwhals and walruses and fish live there too.

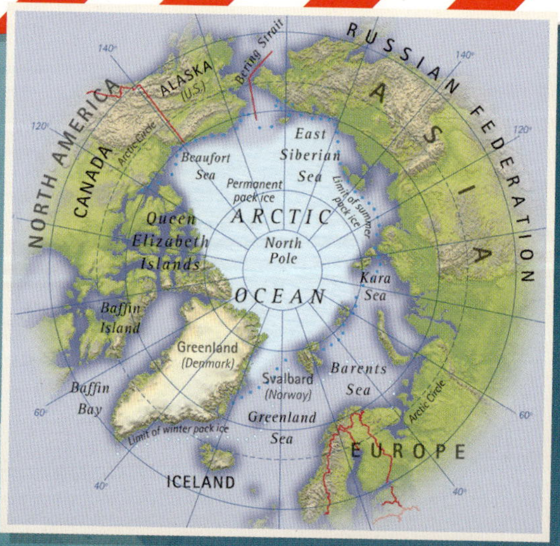

3 Read the text again and write *t* (true) or *f* (false).

1 It rains a lot in the Arctic tundra. ☐
2 There aren't any plants in the tundra. ☐
3 Hares don't eat meat. ☐
4 Narwhals are a type of fish. ☐

4 Match the animals with the features that help them to survive in the Arctic tundra.

1 reindeer

2 narwhals

3 arctic hares

4 walrus

a They have thick fur to keep them warm. In winter, they go south in big groups for food and shelter.

b Their fur is brown in summer and white in winter. This helps them hide from hunters. In winter, they eat moss to survive.

c They are fat and this helps them to keep warm in freezing temperatures. Their two big tusks stop polar bears eating them.

d They are grey, so orca and polar bears can't see them. They eat small fish. They are the only kind of whale that has a tusk. The tusk helps them to fight.

5 Read and answer. Who lives in the Arctic?

Most people who live in the Arctic live in Canada, Alaska and Greenland and they're called *Inuit*. *Inuit* means *people* and the language that people speak the most is called *Inuktitut*.
In the past, the Inuit moved to different places and hunted for seals, walrus and reindeer. In the summer, they slept in tents made of animal skins. In the winter, they slept in shelters made of snow.
Today, the Inuit don't travel as much as before and most of them live in wooden houses. They do still hunt seals, walruses and reindeer for food.

6 Read the text again and write two true or false questions. Ask your partner to answer your questions.

7 Project Make a storyboard with four boxes or a slide presentation with four slides about the Arctic.

- Choose four facts about the Arctic that you find interesting.
- Find or draw an image for each fact.
- Write texts to describe the images in the storyboard or on the slides.
- Present your project to your class.

The Arctic Ocean is the smallest ocean …

The Arctic Ocean is the smallest ocean. It's usually covered in ice.

Get talking

Finding out about holiday plans

1 Work in pairs. Choose a role card.

Student A

You are interested in your friend's holiday plans.

Find out:

- You think he/she is going to Spain. Check.
- How is he/she going to get there?
- You think he/she is going with his/her family. Check.
- What are they going to do there?
- When are they going?

Student B

You want to go on holiday, but you haven't decided anything yet.

Tell your friend:

- where you may/might go
- how you may/might get there
- who may/might go with you
- what you may/might do there
- when you may/might go

2 Act out your dialogue.

Student A

You're going to/with … aren't you?
How are you going to … ?
What kind of things are you going to do?
When is it you're going?

Student B

We may … or we might …
I don't know yet. We may take … or we may go by …
I think so. Last year I went to stay with … but …
If we go to … , we'll … , but if we go to … we might …
I haven't really thought about that yet, but I'd like to try …
We may go at the beginning/end of … , but it depends on my mum's/dad's job.

A review

1 Read the reviews and answer the questions.

Review

SpongeBob Square Pants

Description

It's about a sponge called Bob, who lives in a pineapple under the sea. He's got lots of friends, including fish and other animals. In each episode he has a different crazy adventure.

Who is your favourite character?

Patrick Star, SpongeBob's friend.

Would you recommend it for students of your age? Why (not)?

YES! It's fun to watch. It makes me laugh a lot. I watch it every week and all my friends like it too.

Emma Easthope

Review

ICE AGE: Collision Course

Description

This is the fifth Ice Age film. It's a funny story about four animals: Manny (the mammoth), Diego (the tiger), Scrat (the squirrel) and Sid (the sloth). They live 20,000 years ago when glaciers cover Earth. In this film, they have to save the Earth from meteors.

Who is your favourite character?

Sid, the sloth. He isn't very clever and he makes some silly mistakes, but he's funny.

Would you recommend it for students of your age? Why (not)?

Yes, I would. It's a good story and the animals are great. I've seen it lots of times now online. My dad likes it too.

Zak Robinson

1 Which is a film and which is on TV? Which words in the reviews help you to work it out?

2 Do the reviewers like them?

2 **Write a review of a TV series or a film. Look at the reviews in Activity 1 to help you. Make sure that you include the points below.**

- Name of series/film
- Description
- Who is your favourite character?
- Would you recommend it for students of your age? Why (not)?

Writing tip

When we tell someone about a film or programme that we have seen (even if it was three weeks ago or last year), we often use the present and not the past to tell the story:
It's a film about a man and his son. They live in a hut in the jungle. One day, they notice …

9 The Jurassic Age

1 096 **Listen and say the words. Check with your partner.**

The dinosaurs lived on Earth for more than 160 million years. There were more than 9,000 different dinosaurs and they were found all over the world. The name 'dinosaur' means 'terrible lizard', but not all dinosaurs were dangerous. The last dinosaurs died out about 65 million years ago. No-one knows for sure why this happened.

1. sunrise
2. horizon
3. pond
4. grassland
5. valley
6. bush
7. stream
8. swamp
9. log

BIG QUESTION What do we know about prehistoric times?

2 097 **Read, listen and complete the sentences.**

1 Patrick thinks that they are in the ______________________.
2 Phoebe thinks that they are in the past because ______________________.
3 Patrick isn't scared and wants to ______________________.
4 Phoebe thinks that they should wait behind some ______________________.

3 **Choose a word. Describe it for your partner.**

It's like a little river.

I think that's a stream. Yes?

1 Match the sentence halves. Number the pictures to match the sentences.

1 If I were an inventor,
2 If I had a time machine,
3 If I saw a triceratops,
4 If I saw a T-rex,

a I'd take a photo.
b I'd run back to my time machine.
c I'd make a time machine.
d I'd go back to the time of the dinosaurs.

2 098 Watch, listen and say.

Language focus

If I **had** a time machine,
I'd go back to the past.
But if I saw a dinosaur,
I'd come back very fast.

If I **had** a time machine,
I'd visit the future too.
And if I met the future me,
I'd say 'Well, how are you?'

3 Play *Guess who said it.*

1 099 **Listen and answer the questions. Then sing the song.**

1 What animal body parts are there in the song?
2 Which of the dinosaurs do you think sound friendly / scary / funny / not very nice?

If I were a dinosaur,
I'd hang out, nice and warm,
I'd mess about with all my friends
And poke them with my horns.

I'd like to be a dinosaur.
I think it would be fun
To splash about in muddy swamps
And watch the rising sun.

If I were a big T-rex
With long and pointy claws,
I'd creep up on my friends and then
I'd scare them with my roars.

I'd like to be a dinosaur ...

If I were a pterosaur,
My wings would be so strong,
I'd fly up high and with a roar
I'd drop rocks on everyone.

I'd like to be a dinosaur ...

ALL ABOUT MUSIC: Rap

Rap artists don't really sing. They speak the words of the song quickly and with a musical rhythm. Rapping is a common part of hip-hop music and culture, which started in the African-American communities in New York.

What I think about this song

It's great. It's OK. I don't really like it.

Phonics

2 101 **Listen and say the dialogue.**

Flora Has it got short or long horns, Paul?
Paul Hmm ... it's got short horns.
Flora And big or small jaws?
Paul It's got big jaws ... and sharp claws.
Flora Could it be an albertosaur?
Paul I don't know, Flora, but it's coming towards us!

1 Choose the best answers for you.

Are you a town person or a country person?

1. **Where would you buy a house if you had a lot of money?**
   A In a city. B In a valley by a pond.
2. **What would you do if you saw a bear?**
   A Run away. B Take a photo.
3. **Where would you work if you were older?**
   A In a bank. B In a nature park.
4. **Where would you go for the perfect holiday?**
   A To a theme park. B Camping in the woods.

KEY

Mostly A answers?
You aren't a country person. You like to be in towns with lots of people.
Mostly B answers?
You're a country person. You love animals and nature.

2 Put the words in order to make questions.

1 famous / you / say / if / person / ? / would / What / you / met / a

____

2 live / town / ? / would / Where / if / could / you / chose / you / any

____

3 102 Watch, listen and say.

Language focus

What **would** you **do**,	If I **met** a dinosaur,
What **would** you **say**,	I know what I **would do**.
If you **saw** a dinosaur	I **wouldn't stop** to say 'hello'
Coming your way?	I**'d run** and so **would** you.

4 Work in pairs. What would or wouldn't you do if you met or saw these people and things? Ask and answer.

If I met Beyoncé, I'd …

1 Look at the pictures. Do you know the names of any of these dinosaurs?

2 103 Read and listen to the story to check your answers.

The children looked out from behind the rocks. About ten metres away, there was a huge dinosaur eating from the tops of the bushes. It had a funny-shaped head with three large horns coming out of it. 'Awesome! It's a triceratops!' gasped Alex. 'Isn't it amazing?' and he started to walk slowly towards it. 'Are you mad?' said Patrick in a loud whisper. 'Get back here!' 'Don't be silly,' answered Alex. 'Don't you know anything about dinosaurs? This one's a herbivore. It only eats plants.' 'But Alex, you might scare it! If I were a triceratops, I'd be scared of you!' laughed Phoebe. Alex turned round and pulled a face at her. At that moment, the triceratops lifted its head and looked up and then started walking away quickly. 'What did I say, Alex?' asked Phoebe. 'Look, it's going now!'

However, it wasn't Alex that was scaring the triceratops. 'Look out, Alex!' shouted Phoebe. 'There's something coming towards you.' Alex looked around. Ten small dinosaurs were slowly walking out of the jungle towards Alex. 'Don't worry,' said Patrick. 'They're only small.' One of the creatures opened its mouth and the children noticed lots of tiny sharp teeth. 'I don't think these ones eat plants,' said Alex. 'They're velociraptors.' By now, the dinosaurs were making a circle around him with their mouths open.

Just then, a huge head appeared out of the jungle. It grabbed one of the small dinosaurs and ate it. The others ran away. Alex looked up and saw a big, angry dinosaur. 'It's a T-rex. Run!' he shouted. The children started running, but the T-rex roared loudly and chased after them.

They ran as fast as they could, but the T-rex was catching up with them. It was now only 20 metres behind them and there was nowhere to hide. Suddenly a huge shadow went over their heads. They looked up and saw a giant pterosaur flying down towards them. The dinosaur bird picked up the children in its beak and flew off. They could still hear the angry roar of the T-rex on the ground.

'Oh no, what now?' shouted Patrick. Below them there was a nest with three large baby pterosaurs, waiting with their beaks open. 'We're going to be lunch!' Phoebe shouted back. The flying pterosaur opened its beak and dropped the children. They were just above the nest when a welcome yellow light appeared. They were gone in a flash.

The children landed back in their classroom, where Mr Davis was looking at them. 'Are you three OK?' he asked, sounding worried. 'Why? What happened?' said Alex. 'There was an explosion,' said Mr Davis, 'and then you, Phoebe and Patrick, well … you disappeared for a second or two.'

'Really?' asked Phoebe. 'I don't remember anything. Do you two?' she asked the boys. 'No,' they replied, looking very confused.

Patrick put his hand in his pocket and he pulled out an old bracelet. 'That's strange … *very* strange,' he thought.

3 Use the pictures to help you complete the sentences.

1 
2 
3 
4 
5 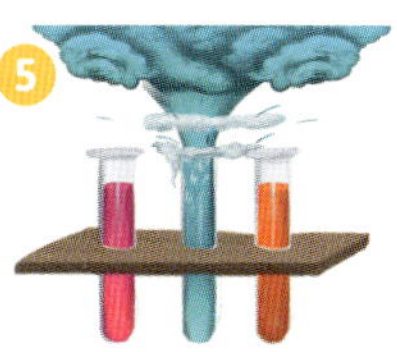
6 

1 The triceratops was eating …
2 The small dinosaurs made a circle around …
3 The T-rex ate …
4 The children were picked up by …
5 Mr Davis told the children about …
6 In his pocket, Patrick found …

4 Help the Time Travellers remember what happened. Where are these things from?

1 
2 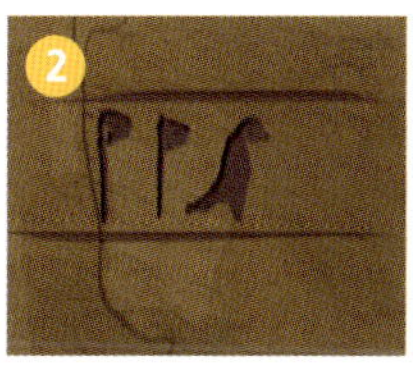
3 
4 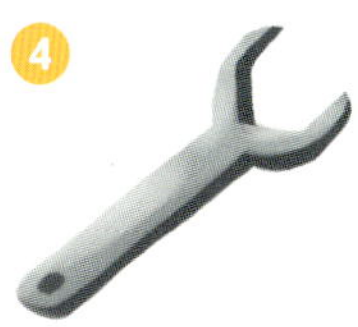
5 
6 

I think the coin is from the island where the children …

1 Look at the pictures. What do you think these animals have in common? Look at the first paragraph of the magazine article and check your answer.

2 Read the magazine article. Which species has been on the Earth the longest?

As old as DINOSAURS

The last dinosaurs walked the Earth about 66 million years ago. We only have their fossils to help us understand what they looked like and how they lived. But did you know there are animals on Earth today that shared the planet with the dinosaurs? Here are four of them.

The platypus is a strange animal which lives only in Australia. It's one of only two mammals that lay eggs. They also have beaks like birds. It spends much of its time in or under water. In 2008, scientists found a platypus bone that was from more than 150 million years ago.

platypus

Turtles are found in warm seas all over the world. The first turtles appeared around 220 million years ago and they have been on Earth since then. They are very good at surviving difficult times. When the weather gets too cold, some turtles hibernate. When it gets too hot, they make holes in mud and wait for the weather to change.

green turtle

Cockroaches are famous for surviving. Scientists say that in the future, they could be the last animals on Earth. They started life here about 360 million years ago, more than 100 million years before the first dinosaurs. The first cockroaches were more than twice as big as the cockroaches of today.

cockroach

Bee fossils are very hard to find, but scientists believe bees first appeared on Earth more than 100 million years ago. The bee fossil was found in amber. Amber is a liquid from trees. Sometimes insects got stuck in the liquid before it got hard.

bee

3 Read the magazine article again. Answer the questions.

Which animal …

1 is smaller now than in the past? ____________________

2 hides to escape from difficult situations? ____________________

3 is only found in one country? ____________________

4 got caught in liquid from trees? ____________________

1 104 Lucy is a member of her local nature club. Listen to the voicemail message and tick ☑ the things she needs to take on her fossil-hunting trip.

1

☐

2

☐

3

☐

4

☐

5

☐

6

☐

2 105 Listen again and answer the questions.

1 What time are they meeting?
2 Where are they meeting?
3 What time will they get back?
4 What is Chris Small's phone number?
5 How much does the trip cost?

3 Discuss in groups.

1 Are you interested in fossils? Are you interested in animals? Why/Why not?
2 Do you think it's important for young people to be interested in nature?

4 Read the riddles and guess the answers.

I lay eggs.
I've got a beak.
But I'm not a bird.
What am I?

I was here before you.
I will be here after you.
What am I?

5 Choose an animal and write a riddle for your classmates to guess.

The Stone Age

What do we know about the Stone Age?

Super fact!

Stone Age people often lived in caves, but they didn't stay in them for long – they moved around a lot. They used animal skins for shelter when there weren't any caves.

1 106 Look, listen and number.

axe

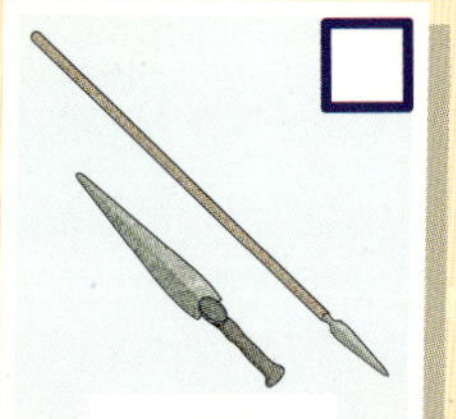
weapon

woolly mammoth

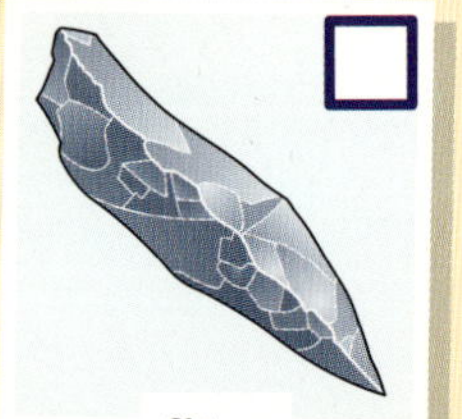
flint

berries

gather

2 Read about the Stone Age and find the words from Activity 1.

Historians use the phrase 'Stone Age' to describe a time when people used stone tools to help them survive. The Stone Age was about 3.4 million years long. It ended when people first started using metal to make tools and weapons.

Stone Age people were hunter-gatherers. This means that they lived in small groups and hunted animals for food. Sometimes they hunted big animals, like woolly mammoths, to eat.

They also looked for plants to gather and eat. They gathered fruit, leaves, berries and birds' eggs too. Most of their food was gathered, not hunted.

For weapons, Stone Age people often used axes with sharp flints on the end of them. Sometimes they cooked food on a fire and cut it with flints, but they ate most of their food without cooking it.

3 Guess what these Stone Age objects a–c are. Read the descriptions and discuss your ideas with a partner.

1 Stone Age people cut down a tree. They made a hole in the middle so they could sit in it. They used it to get across water.
2 Stone Age people killed a reindeer. They took a bone from it. They used a flint to make the bone sharp. They used the sharp bones with some thread to join pieces of animal skins.
3 Stone Age people found yellow clay in the ground. They mixed it with water. They drew dark yellow patterns with it.

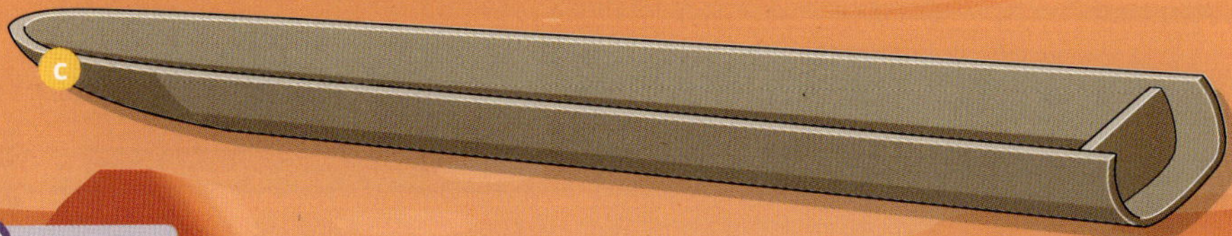

4 107 **Listen. Which stone circle do we hear about?**

Göbekli Tepe

Callanish Standing Stones

Stonehenge

5 108 **Listen again and correct the mistakes in the sentences.**

1 Stone circles were made with very small stones.
2 You can only find stone circles in Africa and Turkey.
3 The oldest stone circle we can see today is in Africa.
4 Stone circles celebrated times when the sun was highest in the sky in winter.
5 The stones were moved using lorries.
6 People used the stones to watch the constellations.

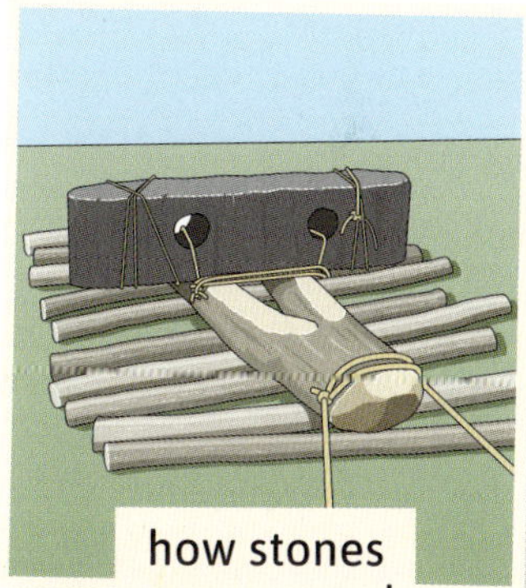
how stones were moved

6 Project **Design and make a stone circle on a paper plate.**

- How many stones will you use?
- Will all the stones be the same?
- Find some small stones.
- Decorate your paper plate and stick the stones on it.
- Name your stone circle and tell your friends what people will do there.

This is my stone circle.
It's called the Friends' Circle.
People will eat and drink there.

Get talking

Presentation for your portfolio

1 109 **Listen to Luke's presentation and find the mistakes in the bullet points.**

Tyrannosaurus rex

- This dinosaur lived 200 million years ago.
- It was green.
- It was 9 metres long.
- It was about 3 metres high.
- It could run at about 50 km/hour.
- It weighed about 2,000 kilos.
- It ate plants.
- Most fossils are found in Australia.

2 **Complete a poster presentation about a dinosaur.**

Find out about it

- Work in pairs. Choose a dinosaur and find out:
  - where people found most fossils of it
  - when it lived
  - what it ate
  - how big it was
  - how heavy it was
  - how fast it could move
  - what colour it was (if scientists know)

Presenting tip

As you prepare, think about the presentations that you have done and seen in your class this year. Which ones worked well? Why? Think how you can use these ideas to improve your presentation.

Prepare it

- Write the text of your presentation first. Then find the main pieces of information to make bullet points for your poster.
- Show the text and the bullet points to your teacher to help you.
- Decide who is going to say what.
- Draw or print out a large picture of the dinosaur.

Present it

- When you present your poster, one of you can point to the bullet points while the other is talking to the class.

An acrostic poem

1 Read these poems, which are called acrostics. What is an acrostic?

Fun and laughter
Running around
In our playground
Enjoy
Not alone
Dreams
Sunshine

Dinosaurs were huge
In a time far away
No people on Earth
One hundred
million years ago
Strong
And dangerous
Under water and on land
Really
Scary

2 Work in groups. Think of ideas for an acrostic poem.

a Make lists of words that start with the same letter.

A: apple, angry, and, art, …
B: blue, before, but, …

b Agree on a word which you all like, for example HOLIDAY, SEASIDE, CHOCOLATE, DRAGONFLY.

c Write the letters of the word in a list down the page.

d As a group, discuss words or word groups that express the idea of your word.

3 Choose ideas and plan your own acrostic. Show your plan to your teacher to help you.

4 Write your acrostic poem. Use colours or add pictures to illustrate your poem.

Holidays are great
On the beach
Lying on the sand
I
D
A
Y

Writing tip

It's always good to check your spelling, but it's even more important if you're writing an acrostic poem or planning puzzles such as crosswords or wordsearches. Use a dictionary to help you if you aren't sure how to spell a word.

Language focus Back to school

Present perfect with *already* / *yet* revision

I **have** (I**'ve**) already ***tidied** my room.
You **have** (You**'ve**) already **met** him.
He **has** (He**'s**) already ***washed** the car.
She **has** (She**'s**) already **made** a cake.
We **have** (We**'ve**) already **seen** this film.
They **have** (They**'ve**) already ***used** it.

I **haven't *repaired** my bike yet.
You **haven't had** lunch yet.
He **hasn't been** to Mexico yet.
She **hasn't read** that book yet.
We **haven't *finished** it yet.
They **haven't *arrived** yet.

Verbs which are regular in the past simple have ***regular** past participles, which look the same as the verbs in the past simple.
Other past participles are irregular. You need to learn these.
There is a list of irregular verbs on page 127 of the Workbook.

1 Complete the sentences with the past participle of the verbs in brackets.

1 Tom has already ______________ his homework. (do)
2 She hasn't ______________ up yet! (get)
3 They haven't ______________ that museum yet. (visit)
4 We've already ______________ some souvenirs. (buy)
5 I haven't ______________ my teeth yet. (brush)
6 He's already ______________ Sue her present. (give)

which / *who* / *where* revision

The tent **which** is near the cliff is ours.
The girls **who** are playing football are in Year 6.
This is the shop **where** they bought the guidebook.

2 Complete the sentences with *which*, *who* or *where*.

1 The woman ______________ won the photo competition is our Art teacher!
2 The house ______________ is opposite the museum is 250 years old.
3 The man ______________ is standing next to the fountain looks like my dad.
4 The park ______________ the girls were playing tennis is closed now.
5 The river ______________ flows through London is called the Thames.
6 The beach ______________ we put up our tent is very windy.

1 The treasure

Present perfect with *for* and *since*

Mum hasn't seen her cousins **for** three years.
We haven't had pizza **for** months!
They've known Daniel **for** six years.
I haven't been very well **since** Thursday.
You've had this bike **since** you were ten.
He has played in our band **since** December.

1 Complete the sentences with *for* or *since*.

1 You haven't tidied your room ____________ a month!
2 We haven't seen any birds on that nest ____________ yesterday.
3 They haven't had a holiday ____________ 2011.
4 She has lived in Chile ____________ three years.
5 I haven't painted any pictures ____________ a long time.
6 My dad hasn't had long hair ____________ he was 16.

How long have you … ?

How long have I/you/we/they **known** Poppy?	**Since** December.
How long have I/you/we/they **been** here?	**For** two hours, I think.
How long has he/she **played** the piano?	**Since** 2012.
How long has it **had** its nest in that tree?	**For** three weeks.

2 Make questions.

1 there / worked / Dad / long / how / has / ?

____

2 we / how / been / here / have / long / ?

____

3 she / how / Mexico / has / in / long / lived / ?

____

4 you / long / phone / have / your / had / how / ?

____

5 a / used / she / long / how / computer / has / ?

____

2 Future transport

need to

We **need to** finish our project tonight. Our teacher wants it tomorrow.
They **need to** listen carefully. It's important.
I don't **need to** help Oliver. He can do his homework easily.
You don't **need to** feed the cat. I've already done that.

1 Complete the sentences with *need to* or *don't need to*.

1 You ______________ help me with the tent, but can you collect wood, please?
2 We ______________ cut the grass. It's too long.
3 You ______________ put on a jumper if you're cold.
4 I ______________ take my ball to the park because Adam's got one.
5 It finishes very late, so they ______________ check when the last train leaves.

will / won't

You**'ll** (**will**) find the key under the vase.
We**'ll** (**will**) have electric cars everywhere in the future.
There**'ll** (**will**) be lots of solar panels.
I **won't** tell you the secret.
We **won't** see you there.
She **won't** play in our team.
There **won't** be any accidents.

2 Complete the dialogues with *'ll/will* or *won't*.

1 A I'm looking for milk, please.
B You ______________ find it next to the cheese, over there.

2 A How can they stop pollution?
B Cars ______________ use electricity in the future.

3 A Don't tell Sandra because it's a surprise.
B OK. I ______________ tell her.

4 A Can I use the laptop, please?
B Not now, but I ______________ give it to you later.

5 A Is Dad home yet?
B No, sorry, and he ______________ be home before bedtime, but you can see him in the morning.

3 Ancient Egypt

Past passive

I **was given** the gold medal for diving.
She **wasn't asked** about the accident.
The tomb **was built** by slaves.
The slaves **weren't paid** any money.

1 **Complete the sentences with the past passive of the verbs in brackets.**

1 Pyramids ______________ by the Mayans in Mexico. (build)
2 Many years ago, sugar ______________ from a big block in the shop. (cut)
3 Before cars ______________, people used boats and carts. (invent)
4 Your room ______________ very well! Go and finish it, please. (not tidy)
5 These football shorts ______________ after the match. Are they yours? (find)
6 Egyptian sledges ______________ by dogs. They used horses and slaves. (not pull)

a lot of / lots of / a few / a little

It was good to see **a lot of** / **lots of** my friends at the party.
There were **a few** students in the cafeteria.
After the flood, there was **a lot of** water in our house.
There was **a little** snow last winter, but we couldn't take the sledges out.

2 **Make sentences.**

1 sky / lot / a / are / in / birds / the / of / there / .
____

2 mistakes / the / a / test / I / few / in / made / .
____

3 lots / party / she / of / at / pizza / ate / the / .
____

4 last / rain / had / lot / a / we / autumn / of / .
____

5 pond / few / a / there / fish / our / in / are / .
____

6 little / my / a / I / pocket / in / have / money / .
____

4 Olympic sports

could (possibility)

I/You/He/She/We/They **could** go to the volleyball match.
I/You/He/She/We/They **could** get a book from the library.
I/You/He/She/We/They **could** have spaghetti tonight.

1 **Complete the sentences with *could* and the verbs from the box.**

help go see ask try put

1 They ______________ to the theatre tonight.
2 I ______________ you to plant the potatoes.
3 We ______________ to get tickets, but there are only a few left.
4 At 2.30, you ______________ the wrestling or the archery.
5 He ______________ Harry to find out about the party.
6 She ______________ up her tent near the river.

Present continuous (future)

I**'m leaving** for Antarctica on Monday.
You**'re giving** an interview tomorrow.
He**'s visiting** his uncle on Saturday afternoon.
She**'s playing** tennis with Amy on Wednesday.
We**'re going** to the match at three o'clock.
They**'re flying** to New York in August.

2 **Complete the sentences with the present continuous of the verbs in brackets.**

1 On Tuesday morning, he ______________ for the weightlifting competition. (train)
2 I ______________ for India on Monday. (leave)
3 We ______________ a match on Saturday morning. (play)
4 Tomorrow morning, she ______________ a presentation. (give)
5 They ______________ to Argentina on Sunday. (fly)
6 My grandma ______________ from her holiday on Friday. (come back)

5 In London

Present perfect with *ever / never*

Have you **ever danced** on ice? **Yes, I have. No, I haven't.**
I **have never seen** an accident. / **I've never seen** an accident.
Has he/she **ever ridden** a camel? **Yes, he/she has. No, he/she hasn't.**
He **has never bought** a new car. / He**'s never bought** a new car.

1 Complete the questions and sentences with the present perfect of the verbs in brackets.

1 I __________ never __________ a unicycle. (ride)
2 __________ you ever __________ a Harry Potter book? (read)
3 __________ he ever __________ a cake? (make)
4 We __________ never __________ Japanese food. (eat)
5 __________ she ever __________ to Paris? (go)
6 Tom __________ never __________ snowboarding. (try)

Present perfect with past simple

Have you **ever seen** an angry polar bear?
No, I **haven't**, but we **studied** them at school!
Has he/she **ever travelled** by elephant?
Yes, he/she **has**, when he/she **was** in Thailand last year.
Have we **ever eaten** crocodile meat?
Yes, we **have**. We **went** to Australia when you were little.

2 Complete the dialogues with the correct forms of the verbs in brackets.

1 A __________ you ever __________ any treasure?
B Yes, I __________. I __________ a ring two years ago. (find)
2 A Dad, __________ Mum ever __________ a famous person?
B Yes, she __________. She __________ a pop star at a party. (meet)
3 A __________ they ever __________ a marathon?
B Yes, they __________. They __________ the Boston marathon last year. (do)
4 A __________ he ever __________ penguins in Antarctica?
B No, he __________, but he __________ some in South Africa four years ago. (see)
5 A __________ they ever __________ Mount Everest?
B No, they __________, but they __________ Mount McKinley in 2013. (climb)

6 Crazy inventions

too many / not enough

There are **too many** cars on the road. People should cycle more.
You didn't pass the test because you made **too many** mistakes.
I can't buy that phone. I **haven't** got **enough** money.
There **isn't enough** water. I can't swim in the pool.

1 Complete the sentences with *too many* or *enough*.

1 You can't get into that bus. There are ______________ people on it already.
2 Sorry, I can't help you. I haven't got ______________ time.
3 Let's not go camping. There are ______________ dark clouds!
4 Oh dear! There aren't ______________ cakes. Have we got any biscuits?
5 I can't make carrot soup. We haven't got ______________ carrots.
6 He never knows which CD to play. He's got ______________ of them!

Can you tell me what this is / does / is for?

Can you tell me **what** this bird **is**? (It's a toucan, from South America.)
Can you tell me **what** this button **does**? (It starts the machine.)
Can you tell me **what** this machine **is for**? (It's for cleaning shoes.)

2 Make questions.

1 what / tell / for / is / me / you / invention / can / this / ?
____
2 does / switch / me / what / can / that / you / tell / ?
____
3 this / you / can / button / for / me / tell / is / what / ?
____
4 you / is / me / what / thing / can / this / tell / ?
____
5 tell / what / lever / that / does / you / can / me / ?
____
6 is / can / tool / me / what / this / you / for / tell / ?
____

7 This is Houston

Gerunds

Learning to ride a horse needs practice.

Travelling to the moon is exciting.

Making a model plane carefully takes time.

Flying in a rocket is amazing.

1 Complete the sentences with the gerund of the verbs in brackets.

1 ________________ to parties is fun. (go)
2 ________________ stories is interesting. (write)
3 ________________ an igloo takes a long time. (build)
4 ________________ at a computer all day isn't good for you. (sit)
5 ________________ the piano well needs lots of practice. (play)
6 ________________ is very good exercise. (swim)

Reported speech

I **said that I didn't like** cheese.

You **said that you played** the guitar.

He **said that he spoke** five languages.

She **said that she enjoyed** looking for treasure.

We **said that we wanted** to build a raft.

They **said that they were** from Peru.

2 Complete the sentences with the past simple of the verbs in brackets.

1 He said that he ________________ fish. (love)
2 She said that she ________________ at a hospital. (work)
3 The aliens said that they ________________ Earth very often. (not visit)
4 He said that he ________________ meat. (not eat)
5 I said that I ________________ a new bike. (want)
6 She said that she ________________ me. (not understand)

8 A cold place

Question tags with *be*

It's hot in here, **isn't it**?

Polar bears are dangerous, **aren't they**?

Spring in Canada isn't very long, **is it**?

Those aren't seal pups on the ice, **are they**?

1 **Complete the sentences with question tags.**

1 The Sphinx is in Egypt, _______________?
2 Most parrots are very colourful, _______________?
3 The Harrisons aren't at home today, _______________?
4 It isn't raining now, _______________?
5 Bears are good at climbing trees, _______________?
6 Mars isn't the smallest planet, _______________?

may / might

I **may** fall if I'm not careful.

You **might** meet a famous footballer at the match.

He **may** go to the museum tomorrow.

She **might** come to France with us.

We **may** have pizza tonight, but I'm not sure.

They **might** drive to New York or they **might** fly.

2 **Make sentences.**

1 tomorrow / go / we / concert / a / to / may / .

____

2 travel / in / might / August / to / Paris / I / .

____

3 year / the / they / moon / fly / next / might / to / .

____

4 on / the / Jane / to / Saturday / may / party / come / .

____

5 weekend / might / the / our / we / grandparents / at / visit / .

____

9 The Jurassic Age

2nd conditional

If I **met** Professor Potts, I'**d ask** him about the homework machine.
If I **were** a dinosaur, I'**d be** a T-rex!
If I **went** into the future, I'**d take** my friends.
If I **saw** a dinosaur, I'**d hide** very quickly.
If I **had** a lot of money, I'**d buy** a castle.

1 **Complete the sentences with the correct form of the verbs from the box.**

be have see meet go

1 If I __________ a robot dog, I'd send it for walks without me!
2 If I __________ a dragon, I'd take a photo.
3 If I __________ J K Rowling, I'd ask her to sign my Harry Potter books.
4 If I __________ an inventor, I'd invent gadgets for astronauts.
5 If I __________ to London, I'd go and see Tower Bridge.

2nd conditional questions

What **would** you **do** if you met an Egyptian mummy?	I'**d run** away.
What **would** you **do** if you saw a polar bear?	I'**d hope** that it couldn't see me.
What **would** you **do** if you had wings?	I'**d fly** to school.
What **would** you **do** if you were a famous singer?	I'**d give** a concert in a big stadium.

2 **Match the questions with the answers.**

1 What would you do if you had a boat?
2 What would you do if you met a monster?
3 What would you do if you saw a mermaid?
4 What would you do if you were in Antarctica?
5 What would you do if you had a rocket?

a I'd swim with her.
b I'd fly to Neptune.
c I'd try to scare it.
d I'd sail down the Amazon.
e I'd look for penguins.